MAUREEN DUFFY

Inherit the Earth

A SOCIAL HISTORY

Hamish Hamilton: London

First published in Great Britain 1980
by Hamish Hamilton Ltd
Garden House, 57-59 Long Acre, London WC2E 9JZ

British Library Cataloguing in Publication Data

Duffy, Maureen
  Inherit the earth.
  1. Jarviss family
  2. Thaxted, Eng. — Genealogy
  I. Title
  929'.2'0942   CS429.J/

ISBN 0-241-10205-7

Printed photolitho in Great Britain
by Ebenezer Baylis & Son Ltd.,
The Trinity Press, Worcester, and London.

Inherit the Earth

Contents

List of Illustrations

Illustrations by Gavin Rowe.

I   Going to Granny's

They got up about eight o'clock because in those days there was
no hurry and they got up one by one because only one could
wash in the scullery sink at a time. They were going to Granny's,
to the country.

Perhaps it's a sign of the inherent matriarchalness of my family
that it was always 'Granny's' they went to although Grandad, my
great grandfather, was no insignificant figure and indeed outlived
his wife and several of his children and grandchildren. He stands
in my mind upright like some archetypal tree or column, Samuel
Jarvis, born 1848, died 1935, photographed in a family group in
summer time in his daughter's London garden, before my time.

But in 1910 when Maud, the mother of one of the children,
who are the focus of the snapshot that shows Samuel, was herself
only the same age as the century, it was Granny's they were going
to, even though Granny and Grandad didn't live there now but
a few streets away from them in Stratford and, as the eldest of the
girls still at school, it was her job to help with washing and
dressing the smaller ones. Of course there was Chug, only two
years older and so not yet at work, but he was a boy and couldn't
be expected to do girls' jobs. He would help to carry the luggage.

Once she had gone alone with father; she was father's favourite.
But she had missed her mother and the others and cried with a
headache because she wanted to come home. Going all together
was different. They had their breakfast of bread and margarine
with jam, bought a ha'pporth at a time in a basin, and tea with
skimmed, tinned milk, except for mother who had a farthings-
worth of cowsmilk for her tea. Sometimes as a special treat they
had a sop: a thick slice of bread cut into squares and put in a cup
or mug with margarine on the top and bottom layers of bread,
and with a sprinkling of salt and boiling water poured over just
to moisten it. Sometimes too the elder boys, Skippy and Tich,

1

would have got up early before work and been to the big baker's with a pillowcase for a shillingsworth of stale bread that, with luck, would have a currant or malt loaf among its assorted horseshoe, cottage and Dutch shapes. Damped a little and heated in the oven it came up like fresh, while what was finally left over was soaked for bread pudding.

Seconds were a necessary part of subsistence: broken biscuits, specked apples from the greengrocer's and bruised oranges to make father's wine; offal of all sorts, heads, liver, tripes, tongues. Yet even so they were undernourished, pasty-faced and consumptive. A week in the country at Granny's would do them all good. It was father's annual unpaid week's holiday when the railway works, where he was a blacksmith's striker, were shut. Nothing was to be gained by staying at home when they could travel free on his railwayman's pass and be fed by mother's family. They were dressed in their best, all made by mother, patterned print frocks and coats, with cotton socks and button boots for the girls and sailor suits with more boots for the boys. Only Skippy, employed as an office messenger-boy, wore shoes. Father mended them all, including his own well brushed black boots.

As they left the house the street seemed quieter than usual. There was only an occasional hiss from a cooling boiler, not the clang of shunting, of metal on metal and the warning notes of train whistles from behind the Works' wall opposite. They walked through the backchats to Stratford Station and rode to the bellowing iron and glass cathedral at Liverpool Street where the trains snorted and roared like brass bulls. Dingy Owl, the eldest of the three last children, nicknamed after a neighbour's dismal fowl, moped and grizzled as she always did. They were all glad to be on their train and pulling out, soothed by the repetitive rhythm of wheels on rails, seeing, out of the smutted windows, the fields and trees begin, summer fields of ripening wheat or pastures where cows swished their tails in the fly humming shade and stared at the train. Maud paid particular attention to the woodwork and upholstery. Father had put her name down to join him inside the works in the carriage shop when she was old enough.

For mother it was going home. The journey to Elsenham took just over an hour, eked out by a few sweets, and there, if no one

2

had come to meet them with pony and trap, they took Coe's horse-drawn public carrier for the last few miles to Thaxted which still had no station of its own. Here mother had been born in 1872, Minnie Lydia, daughter of Samuel and Lydia Jarvis, whose maiden name before she married in 1870 was Gilder.

Granny was not yet seventeen when she married, since when she had borne what John Donne called a 'mast of children', dropped like acorns every three years so that she was still bearing them when her eldest daughter married and began to bear in her turn but at intervals of eighteen months. Families are tidier now; the generations more distinct. Then uncles and nephews might be of an age, at play together. Before the choice given by contraception only abstinence or infertility limited the size of a family. Both states were subjects of speculation, gossip and often shame, particularly in a small community. The shame fell mostly on the man since infertility was read as impotence.

Seven long years I made his bed
Six of them I lay beside him
And this morning I rose with my maidenhead
For still he had no courage in him.
    O dear O what shall I do
My husband got no courage in him.

At the Dunmow Flitch trial in 1899 no one brought home the bacon because the jury of six maids and six bachelors decided 'that there was an absence of love when there was an empty stomach', and the contenders were childless.

Samuel Jarvis had no need to worry, with ten evidences of his potency. It's hard now to imagine thirty years of inevitable childbearing, and the life, and constantly repeated fear of death, that went with it. It was only natural, and besides they were used to it, the arguments run, but once given the choice women abandoned centuries of female custom and practice in a generation. The plump little girl in the summer photograph was to be Maud's only child.

Maud herself was number six in the family. Her second name was Lydia, after her mother and grandmother. Those visits to Granny's have become for her a Golden Age of leaves and sunlight, woods and fields under that even softer luminescence, the remembered carelessness of childhood. Here there were

3

multicoloured flowers and unspecked fruit, innumerable houses to visit of Jarvisses and Gilders, all anxious to see Minnie's children go back to the city with colour in their cheeks.

Thaxted, like many other Essex parishes, is a star with attendant planets, small hamlets which are mere clusters of houses that sometimes seem to have no reason for their setting down just there as if a child with more artistic than practical sense had been at play. Lydia had been born in one of these, Cutler's Green, a tiny medieval housing estate now down a lane that seems to be going nowhere.

It's hard to see why the Cutlers should have concentrated themselves there, apart from the good water supply that must have been useful in smelting, and perhaps it's just a fiction and the name is really a corruption of Beaucondre, a family that owned property thereabouts, since a fourteenth-century version of the name gives it as Biewcoteler-grene. But it's right that the cutlers should have their memorial even if folk memory distorted something else to give it to them. It was, as it so often is, being just to a real truth, for the cutlers have left their hallmark on Thaxted though they have been gone to Sheffield over five hundred years. It was they who made the prosperity that built the magnificent church with its chapel to their patron saint, Laurence, because of his bizarre death roasted on a griddle. It was they who made their part of the town a borough in fact though without a charter until they were mostly gone and the town in decay. In the poll taken about 1381, cutlery and metal working account for a third of the male jobs.

History, and family history is no exception, is full of small and great ironies. Lydia's family, which found itself living in Cutler's Green by the middle of the nineteenth century, bears a name, Gilder, derived from metal-working, if not precisely from cutlery, yet they were the foreigners in Thaxted for they had only been there just over a hundred years. When Maud went home to Granny's it was Cutler's Green that she remembered and passed on to the younger children who were hardly old enough to remember it for themselves, and in turn it was passed to the next generation which is mine.

Maud Lydia, Minnie Lydia and Lydia, and behind her another Lydia, her aunt: they stretch like a daisychain of girls back almost to the eighteenth century.

4

Lydia, lovely maid, more fair
Than milk or whitest lilies are,
Than polisht Indian ivory shows,
Or the fair unblushing rose.

Prosaically at home they were more often 'Tin Liddy'.

Lydia and Samuel were the first of my direct ancestors to be able to read and write since over a century and a half. Proudly they signed the marriage register and proudly Lydia recorded the birth of her first child, my grandmother, Minnie Lydia. Perhaps because I am a writer I find the records of their own births with 'The Mark of Sarah Gilder, Mother', and 'The Mark of Sarah Jarvis, Mother', moving and at the same time frightening. Suppose Samuel and Lydia had never taken up that baton to pass down to me and I was unable to ply my chosen craft. Would Minnie and her husband, George, or even their daughter, my mother, have somehow got hold of it to pass on? I have to be grateful to them for their unaccustomed hours in the schoolroom, hours when their chilblained fingers could hardly hold the strange new tools or when the warm sun and the woods invited beyond the schoolroom window, and to their mute parents who made the sacrifices to school them, those two Sarahs and the two Josephs, their husbands, doing without their children's labour and finding the pennies for their school fees before elementary education was compulsory and free.

Perhaps it was just this education that made it possible for Samuel and Lydia to leave Thaxted and take the leap into the dark that their migration to London must have been. By the time their eldest child, Minnie, was old enough to marry they had left their birthplace and had settled in urban Essex, Stratford in West Ham, ironically in a street named after the little town next to Thaxted that the Gilders had originally come from, Dunmow Road.

There was nothing particularly remarkable in Samuel's flit to town. He was one of nearly 170,000 agricultural labourers and shepherds who took that road in those twenty years. A series of disastrous seasons combined with cheap imported wheat caused farmers to switch from arable to livestock farming, which needed fewer workers, while at the same time the average wage in the Eastern part of the country fell from 12s 11½ a week to 11s 0½.

Yet over two and a quarter million people still stayed on the land during a period described by the Royal Commission appointed to inquire into it as 'a general calamity'. It must have taken courage and desperation to be one of the roughly seven per cent who gambled that there was work to be had in the already overcrowded London described by Mayhew ten years before. One day the farmer he worked for told him there would be nothing for him the next day. 'Right,' said Samuel, 'then I shan't be back.'

Since John Norden drew his map of Essex in the 1590s, the road from Cambridge has led down past Thaxted straight to Stratford and Queen Matilda's Bow Bridge carrying the road across the River Lea and on into London. It must have seemed the natural site for the Great Eastern's fan of railway lines to spread out from. There was plenty of spare land in the marshes to build the sidings and works on. From the 1840s the population began to grow without any facilities to deal with it. Fever, smallpox and cholera chased each other in successive epidemics. 'The whole parish is divided and subdivided by open ditches and sewers and in no instance — and I perambulated nearly the whole area of the parish — did I find one that was not horribly filthy and offensive. The system of cesspools is universal, they are seldom emptied and are overflowing. If the tenants complain they receive notice to quit. New houses are springing up in prodigious numbers with a total absence of system. Nothing could be worse than the state of the poorer dwellings,' wrote a government health inspector in the 1850s. There was no street lighting, inadequate water supply and in some places the potholes in the roads were so large and full of water that pigs wallowed in them.

Still the Klondike rush continued, increasing sevenfold in the next thirty years, so that, by the time Samuel and Lydia with their eldest children reached there, West Ham had become the ninth largest town in England and Wales, on the point of applying for that borough status that Thaxted, with its population of just under two thousand, had been given three hundred years before.

Conditions had improved a great deal in the last thirty years and Stratford was no longer the frontier town it had been, though out of every five children born one still died before the age of two. The main streets were paved and gaslit and there were lavatories in the gardens, always known as the backyard, connected to the main sewage system. But epidemics still swept through the little streets and the air was heavy with soot, and chemicals from the hundreds of factories which had sprung up around the railway, and combined with the fog from the marshes into a killer miasma that wrapped itself around the lungs.

Yet in a strange way Stratford remained Essex. Even that use of 'backyard' harks back in Essex terminology to at least the sixteenth century, when Samuel's ancestors were bequeathing their 'yards and outyards with all their appurtenances' to their heirs. The houses too, though grander than those in Thaxted, with their three bedrooms, one room for the parents, one for the boys and one for the girls, still echoed in shape and height the cottages the migrants had been born in and that had changed hardly at all since Queen Elizabeth I rode by them.

It's interesting to speculate what grapevine carried the information that there was work in Stratford up to the borders of Cambridgeshire. Perhaps someone had already made the journey and sent back news. Certainly, even when I was a child, the part of West Ham they had come to, Stratford New Town, a grid of railwaymen's cottages stretching east from the works' wall, was peopled with Essex names: Stally, Cracknell, Goodeve, Siggers, Hutchings. It was in the works and on the lines that Samuel, his children and grandchildren were to find jobs among those 'princes of the working class', the railwaymen, until the works themselves were closed down after the Second World War and the protestors carried their symbolic coffin in a vain funeral procession to the Town Hall, burying a hundred years of labour.

Samuel and Lydia had always meant their stay in town to be temporary and they had intended from the first that one day they would go home, even if only like aborigines or elephants to die. Once Samuel reached compulsory retiring age there was nothing to keep them. They returned to their beginning, taking some of their children with them but leaving Minnie, now married with children of her own, behind. Did she weep to see them go? No one remembers. There's only one record of her tears: when she learnt of the death of her favourite brother Frank, the blue marine, drowned before the Great War at Malta.

From her, and presumably from her parents, comes a family

tradition of never showing emotion or discussing feelings, a stoicism valuable in distress but emotionally and intellectually restrictive. So many things were taboo, not for discussion, only the bare fact mentioned in the undertone of censorship: 'She died of cancer; he ran off with another woman.' Otherwise all the crises of life, including and particularly sex and death, took place in a throwaway blitz spirit. Nothing was said straight if it could be turned by irony or wry wit or, by the time of my childhood, encased in a shield of slang that at once made it more verbally exciting and drained it of dangerous emotion.

The slang itself was a compound of Essex and cockney with dashes of Hindu and American. Money for instance, our lifeblood that ebbed rapidly away through the week until Thursday payday gave a new shot in the arm, was always 'dough' or 'spondulics' 'tin' or 'hapence'. With such belittlements we kept it in its place and reduced its power over us. It was a process similar to that which called fairies 'the Good People' to turn away their malignancy, or the Furies of Greek mythology, those snaky vengeful harpies, 'the kindly ones'.

By the same process as it were in reverse, Maud and her brothers and sisters protected themselves from any excess of family affection, any 'sloppiness' or 'soppiness', by nicknames. Death and illness were ever present. The elder girls were consumptive. Father sent away hard-earned shillings for patent medicines that might do them good, and flowers came from Aunt Daisy, mother's sister, in Cutler's Green, the first time Maud had seen wallflowers that weren't a uniform rusty blood colour, when Maria as she was known, the eldest girl, actually christened Minnie after her mother, first fell ill.

> Wally, wally wallflowers
> Growing up so high
> We're all pretty maidens
> And we shall have to die
> Excepting only . . .

the children sang in their games, not knowing that it was to be 'excepting only Maud' as all the other girls sickened and died.

The wallflowers came every spring in a box, filling the house with their scent to chase away death and sweeten the air. They remained my own mother's favourite flower though I don't believe she ever knew why. The wallflowers were all gone of course by the time the family reached Aunt Daisy's in the summer when they went to Granny's but there were other flowers that they brought home in great armfuls, and honey from Aunt Daisy's bees. Honey and blossoms with the children wandering among them — Arthur and Frank in their blue and white suits, Maud in her best cotton print and the three youngest girls in their pinafores — conjure up a Victorian painting of children and flowers, yet turn the canvas and it is backed with another popular subject, Death and the Maiden. *Fading Away* it was called in the photograph version where the girl lies a long time dying propped up in a day bed while her mother sits at her feet and father looks out of the window to hide an impotent despair.

Maud herself was to despair as her sisters drooped and died, never believing that in her the family's inheritance of old bones, once you were safely out of dangerous childhood and youth, was strong and she would outlast them all.

The visits to Granny's stopped with the beginning of the war and father's sudden death in 1915, at the age of forty-seven, leaving mother with four children still at school. His long illness had irked him and made him a bad patient so that even Maud, his favourite, wept less than for the death of her eldest sister a year before. For father's funeral she had a beautiful black silk hat which suited her fair hair and a black costume, for she was now a young lady working at the print works where sister Maisie was a vellum sewer. They took their dinner to heat up in the staff kitchen and sat at their workbench eating suet pudding with golden syrup and telling the story of last night's film.

There was one more visit to Granny's when the war was over, to a family wedding, when they all rolled home singing on the top of a farm cart under the moon, and then no more for many years until, when at last she went again, Aunt Daisy shook her head at her in amazement. 'But Maud you're so old!' For them both time had stood still. Yet Thaxted hadn't been forgotten. It had gone on existing in the family imagination, passed on to the next generation as it had been in Maud's childhood like enchanted ground.

Surprisingly mother herself kept her countrywoman's appearance of rosy cheeks and round apple smiling face even through winters of peasoupers and scrubbing the railway offices and stairs on cold dark mornings after her husband's death. The words themselves that describe her belong to an age buried by the Second World War which she never lived to see, her wars being the Boer War so far away, and the Great War that took her abroad for the only time in her life, with her eldest son's young wife, to visit him when he was in hospital with pneumonia in France.

The beginning of the new age is perhaps best symbolized by the family's first gramophone, with its rose-coloured horn and light-oak wooden box, and a small stock of records: 'The Whistler and his Dog'; 'Under the Double Eagle'; 'Take a Pair of Sparkling Eyes'. It was the front runner of the technological revolution and I'm glad that it came in the form of an adult's toy that made them music and set them dancing. Maud herself could set them singing at the family piano topped by its glass-domed set piece of wax flowers, fruit and birds and a set of wooden reins made by father when he was little coiled reverentially round its base. When mother's marine brother came to visit them in his spruce uniform with its red pillbox hat, they had a singsong, as they did at all family gatherings, a custom kept up by Maud for the rest of her life.

In my mind they exist like the wax petals and plumage under that dome, set apart by an almost invisible barrier that lets me see still but not touch although I can almost hear the piano. Like the gramophone I recreate sounds past from memory, and then superimpose them on an even earlier time. The difference between the mechanical memory of the gramophone and the struck immediacy of the piano is a measure of the difference between that last age and this, even though it took as much as another forty years before the gramophone was joined in the family by its technological siblings: the wireless, telephone, vacuum cleaner, fridge, television, washing machine, to alter the whole physical mode of life.

It's fashionable to bewail this loss of immediacy. We live now in a world almost as different from the old one as the first fish that hauled itself out of the water to waddle the shore on its fins must have found, an elemental difference. It would be easy to romanticize those lives that were hard and often hungry. It would be easy too to make the experiment of living as they did but few of us do it. However much we lament the lost virtues of wartime, we do prefer peace. To break the ice in the morning kettle may be fun on a camping holiday but not every winter morning before getting to work at six.

Mother's early hours made it possible for her to spend the day at home mixing and boiling the suet pudding for Maud and Maisie to take to work and the dinners for the children still at school, who would come home and weep if they saw no big black pudding pot on the boil. Then there were their clothes for her to wash, standing in the yard with scrubbing board and galvanized bath. Here town and country met. Her sisters, married in Thaxted, cooked and washed as she did, though their clothes weren't rimed as black. Bed, she would say, was the best place in the world.

Her parents, Samuel and Lydia, must have gone back to live in the country about the time that Maud's father died, when Samuel reached his sixty-fifth year. He was to return to Stratford to live with his daughter after Lydia's death and be present to be snapped among his great-grandchildren. Then he went home to die too and be buried beside Lydia, 'reunited' as their tombstone reads. But on that first return home he took up a series of new jobs, one as a slatelayer, and so described himself at the wedding of his youngest son, Walter, who because he was a cripple was a snob, in the literal not the social sense of that word, which survived in Essex and East London with its original meaning of cobbler. Since he was unfit to be a labourer Walter became a craftsman. Eventually he had his own shop in Newbiggen St, which was newbuilt in Elizabeth I's time.

It was one of the houses Maud visited all those years later when Aunt Daisy, separated now from her bees to whom she had told everything and living in one of the almshouses, shook her head over Maud's great age. The house in Newbiggen was even smaller than Maud's own house in Dunmow Road, for, by one of the turns of history, this time the blitz, she was back in the street from which mother had been married. Yet like hers Walter's house had a piano dwarfing the little living room, as did all the front rooms of my childhood. In the backyard was a thatched lavatory like a dwarf's cottage with two seats side by side and a latched door. The houses which had begun as double-fronted new dwellings had been split at some date into labourers' cottages and minute shops.

The journey through time is cheaper but not necessarily easier than that through space. For continents and rivers you have periods and trends but the basic stuff is the same: the unfamiliar or familiar in a strange dress, so that at the end you emerge with some old perceptions strengthened and others changed. As I moved through my time journey backwards from the ten-year-old Maud going to Granny's, I found myself held and intrigued not because these were my ancestors but because of the continuous thread I unravelled as I went, the historical chain of cause and effect, modified in its unwinding by chance and personal choice, which in its turn is modified by cause and effect and chance. Often my strongest emotions were that classic pair: anger and pity.

The cottage to which Samuel brought his sixteen-year-old bride, after a wedding in the parish church that cost him seven shillings and six pence and two loaves of bread, was at Mill End, the bottom of the town on the Dunmow road, next to the Star and near the sweet factory where some of my cousins, their descendants, still work. Samuel was twenty-two, a labourer like his father Joseph. The witnesses at their wedding were his brother Thomas and Hannah Wren. Six months later they too were married and Lydia and Samuel were the witnesses. Did they meet at the wedding as best man and chief bridesmaid who were traditionally at risk in this situation? Did Hannah catch Lydia's bouquet when it was thrown at the guests? Or were they all four friends, already walking out in couples, and determined to be witnesses at each other's weddings?

Hannah and Thomas had also signed the register and this common literacy must have gone part of the way to set Lydia and Samuel free to go to London. They had discovered the letter. No longer would they or their parents have to wait for months for news until someone came bringing it by word of mouth. Now they could write and although the two Josephs and the two Sarahs, their parents, couldn't read it themselves there were children still at home in Thaxted who could and write back in return. To those who wanted to leave a closely dependent family group, writing was the necessary liberator.

It was of course resisted. An Essex dialect poem of the 1890s puts the case.

Me, nao, sir, I don't howd 'ith these Board Schools;
    They larn the boys too much, my thinking, now.
An' what I see, there's jest as many fools
    As when thay put the young uns to the plough.

I howd 'ith larning, mind, but let 'em larn
    Saime way as I did, not that stuff o' theirs.
Larn 'em the proper way to thetch a barn,
    Leern 'em the way to sao a field o' tares.

Geoggerfy! Now what on arth's the sense
    A larnin of 'em how the moon go roun'?
An' all about Ameriky an' France,
    An plaices tother side o' Lunnon town?

My booy he came to me the tother night,
    'D'yer knaow,' he say, 'the World an' you an' me
Are tarnin' on our axles — sich a raite
    You woon believe? But there, tha's right,' says he.

I tarned he on his axles, you be boun',
    I cop he one. That maide me reg'ler riled,
That fairly did. The Warld a tarnin' roun'!
    To hear sich stuff an' nonsense from a child!

To that writer's mind it didn't matter what they 'larned' the
girls, they simply don't figure, and it's much to the credit of those
parents, of for instance Lydia, who sent their girls to school when
they had no need to. It may be said that they were aping their
betters or glad to get the child out from underfoot but in fact a
girl's labour was very valuable in a house full of children. There
were a hundred jobs she could do and it was a real sacrifice on
her mother's part to part with her for school. Lydia herself was
driven to send her youngest son out to work when he was only
ten and times were particularly hard. And there perhaps lies the
root of our matriarchy. It was the women who were the
economists, the managers, and to be a good or bad manager
meant the difference between survival and collapse for the family.
Even a good husband who brought his wage packet straight
home and passed it across the tea-table unopened could do little
to augment his income. Rates were fixed, overtime was chancy

13

and on a rota system. Hours were long and work hard and there was little opportunity for moonlighting. All this gave the man a certain irresponsibility. He had done his bit. It was up to her what she made of what he could give her. If she scrimped and stitched, boiled up remains, made puddings, scrubbed, all might be well. The man's part was to get a job and keep it.

The poem is very ambiguous in its attitudes. It doesn't condemn the speaker for his rejection of *These New-fangled Ways*. While it laughs at him a little it also respects him as the upholder of the traditional even where it means clouting his son for putting forward a view generally at this date accepted by the middle classes as a rational explanation of the universe. The resentment of geography and astronomy as fit subjects for the sons of labourers comes across strongly. The clue is of course in the implications of such knowledge. If a peasant boy knew about France and America he might as a man go to London. His horizon had been extended. And if he knew that the moon turned on its axis, if he knew the mutability of the earth, he might no longer accept the immutability of the social order, might ask that that too might pivot a little, if not pirouette.

The theme is also an interesting example of the generation gap, thought to be a recent invention, and of its exploitation for political ends. Let the young go. The old wisdom, practical craftsmanship, was the best. It is a temptation to which we constantly return and may indeed be truly the Englishman's vice. Fewer labourers were needed and the jobs could perhaps be best done by the elderly and docile. Those with the new-fangled learning should find themselves work in the towns, as Samuel did, and not stay to cause trouble by asking for higher wages and better conditions, by calling tithes and suchlike into question under the influence of liberal political agitators like William Ewart Gladstone.

> Warty, he talk to 'em to rights las night —
>   I never h'ard a chap a talkin' sao.
> He say the lan an that is ourn by right,
>   But bless yer, I din knaow.

These poems were written by the editor of an Essex county paper. There's no record of whether their subjects, the labourers, read them or, if they did, what they thought of the picture of themselves they found in those lines. Among other things the ballads show them as barely reformed alcoholics, as still afraid of the Old 'Un and yet prepared to tie a half-witted child to a tree and frighten it quite to death with a sheeted ghost, as a mixture of political naivety and peasant cunning. Perhaps these verses took away their taste for poetry. Certainly in my own family such a taste was actively scorned as a lying waste of time and had to be fought for with tenacity and a kind of arrogance that dared to know better.

History on the other hand was respected as truth, even though it was a partial and in some ways irrelevant truth of monarchs and battles. Behind the veil of an unrecorded social past lay a national past in which in some way we partook through virtue of the two world wars. Agincourt and Waterloo were part of a continuum that contained Ypres and Alamein and were therefore ours as much as the kings' and generals'. We knew the dates of English victories — seemingly there were no defeats since the Norman conquest — but not our own past because surely there was nothing to it. None of us had ever done anything worth remembering or writing down. We were as anonymous as coral polyps making up the great reef of society, and had always been. That too was the truth.

And like those polyps we didn't even know how long we had been part of that anonymity, nor whether when Maud went to Granny's the place that she visited, Thaxted, was just one stop in a long series of migrations. We had of course lived there for donkeys' years but these can be as short as a decade or as long as a lifetime. Nor did we know what process had fetched us up against the wall of Stratford works like the flotsam at the tideline we picked over on trips to the seaside and that was more curious and beautiful than we were.

Maud herself was a pretty, comely girl. At about sixteen she was photographed in a local studio, Scotts of Leytonstone Road, with the two youngest girls standing behind her as she sits on a white painted seat. Behind them is an artificial backdrop of a wooded valley and meandering stream and underfoot the formal pattern of the lino. The little girls wear thin cotton dresses made by mother, with crocheted collars, black stockings and boots. Their long dark hair is brushed and shining. Maud wears a dress of white voile and one elegant shoe is thrust forward as she sits.

The back of the picture turns it into a postcard with directions in French and English, perhaps a special arrangement for wartime for it was abandoned a few years later when the girls were photographed again, with the same seat and lino but a cottage backdrop with roses round a wooden porch whose pillars were turned like table legs.

Samuel and Lydia had been photographed in that very studio about the turn of the century: she seated in black silk with a fob watch or oval locket pinned to her bosom and the chain looping over the shiny black slopes, her white hair swept up, her gaze out at the world massively calm; he standing like an eagle with a fierce bright look, a face like Freud's above the winged shirt collar, a loose tweed jacket and black trousers. Perhaps it was taken in 1900 to celebrate their thirtieth wedding anniversary. If so they had just buried the last of their children, baby Maud, died of fever, in a tiny coffin, and her namesake, Maud Lydia, was not yet a year old.

The human lifespan if lived to the full is long enough to see a recognisable segment of history unfurl. Samuel was born in the year of the Chartists' Great Petition and died in the Depression. He lived through what might be called the mechanical revolution yet by the standards of his great grandchildren his life, and Lydia's, was one of material poverty and deprivation, even though he was at last given back the right to vote, which his ancestors had lost, and even though he always managed somehow to find himself a job. Lydia was born in the Crimean War and died in the Jazz Age, and that perhaps gives some measure of the change their joint lives had seen. But it was a change that, in any real sense, had left them untouched.

Not surprisingly Samuel's favourite song was about money.

I love a shilling
A jolly old shilling.
I'll lend a penny on't
I'll take another one
I'll take money home to the wife . . .

he would sing sitting in his old armchair when he came home from work and they were all laughing together. Mrs C. S. Peel, in her *10/- a head for House Books*, about 1898, estimated that servants could be fed for '8/6 per head for a sufficiency of wholesome food'. This didn't allow for meat suppers every night and was therefore only suitable for a smallish household where not many menservants were kept. It was a sum not far short of Lydia's resources to feed the whole family.

And when even that dried up, with his forced retirement in 1914, Samuel gave his children remaining at home his ultimatum: they could stay in the city or go back to their parents' roots with them. Samuel and Lydia couldn't know of course how far back those country roots stretched. They didn't know that they had been embedded in Thaxted for five hundred years.

II   *Witchcraft*

The Jarvisses came first, though I can't say exactly where from. They weren't there in the fourteenth century of plague and revolution. Some time in the fifteenth they must have arrived or perhaps the beginning of the sixteenth but the records are scanty, the occasional surviving lists creased or stained tantalisingly at possible variants of the name that had come over with some obscure holder of horses in William the Conqueror's army, Gervase, or perhaps with someone who had made his way across once the fighting was safely over, hearing that the pickings were good in the service of the new earls, his compatriots.

It's hard to see why the name of one of a pair of dubious martyrs, dug up under St Ambrose's dream-directed orders outside Milan in the fourth century, should have become so popular throughout France or why the martyr should have had a Germanic name in the first place. As with their transmutation of Henri into Harry, the English soon began to change Gervase to Gervys, Jervice and finally Jarvis. The name means slave of the spear and it's an interesting coincidence that the name of the Saxon thane who owned Thaxted before the Conquest, Wisgar, means spear-wise. In many respects there was little to choose between the cousins, conqueror and conquered.

William I gave Thaxted, along with much else, to Robert Fitzgislebert, son of the Earl of Brion. Gilbert, his son, was made Earl of Clare, and after his line had died out in 1314 the property was subsequently divided, not to be reunited until it passed into the royal hands and was eventually given to Henry VIII's undertreasurer, Sir John Cutt. It's because so many of the court rolls and rental accounts of the manor have survived that it's possible to trace much of the history of the district and its people.

This isn't so, however, for records before the Peasants' Revolt in 1381. As elsewhere, the inhabitants of Thaxted took the chance presented by the rebellion to burn the earlier records which gave the fullest details of the lord's rights and their obligations, not, it's been suggested by K. C. Newton in his study of the remaining fourteenth-century accounts, because the peasants here were particularly unfree but precisely because they had got a measure of freedom and had begun to commute their services to the lord into money payments, largely, I suspect, because of a series of absentee overlords who were, as classical capitalists, more interested in rents in cash and kind than in maintaining a local feudal presence. The level of legal enclosure of pieces of the domain lands by tenants, subsequently recognised by the fixing of a rent, is very noticeable and suggests a distant and rather lax hand.

The prosperity of the cutlery industry in Thaxted, which gave so many of the inhabitants an alternative source of income and which is clearly evidenced in local deeds, the Calendar of Close Rolls and the return of the very poll tax that set off the Peasants' Revolt, must have helped in the surge for freedom that destroyed the old manorial records. Why then did the cutlers leave? No one knows for sure but I am prepared to offer a theory and that is that they left partly because of the lack of political and social progress in the town after the rebellion.

It was the Essex men at Mile End who were the first to be given charters of freedom by the boy king Richard II and to return home believing they had achieved their ends. But these charters were soon revoked as being made under duress, and in any case the local lords refused to recognise them, claiming that the crown had no constitutional ability to give away their property. Though Thaxted had been granted the right to hold two fairs a year, which would have provided a market for the cutlers' wares, it had no charter to allow the town to develop fully and no resident lord to push it forward in the hope of increased returns to himself. A survey taken twelve years after the rebellion shows that the manor was still run on a mixture of work, fees and rents and the series of court rolls shows fines for broken hedges, undug ditches and poor maintenance and the constant exaction of small fees whenever properties changed hands by will or assignment. When the town was finally given a charter there was a lengthy struggle with the then lord Sir John Cutt. In contrast

Sheffield, besides having the enormous benefit of its local iron, had been given a charter by its own lord as early as the thirteenth century with freedom to develop and to amass wealth and property in the hands of its governing burgesses.

Thaxted became a backwater. There were still cutlers in the town but the industry as such didn't develop, even though it might be thought that the French wars and the Wars of the Roses would have stimulated the making of blades of every kind. As the cutlers declined, however, the woollen industry grew, though once again on an individual basis rather than as a locally organised trade that might have saved the town from that decay it was in when it applied for its charter. By Essex standards it didn't even become a secondary cloth town, like Coggeshall or Dedham, although as a cottage industry some aspect of the trade was to be important to Thaxted people for the next three hundred years.

The manor itself finally passed through the hands of several royal ladies until it reached Catherine of Aragon and was given to Sir John Cutt. Meanwhile parts of it had been leased to wealthy tenants by overlords whose names read like the cast list to a Shakespeare history play: Oxford, Mortimer, Spencer, Bohun, and including a Maud, Countess of Gloucester, fore-shadowing the return of that name to Thaxted so much later. Decayed though it was since the days of the cutlers and the building of the great church, the town must still have seemed a place of opportunity, for towards the end of the fifteenth century many new names began to appear among the tenants and taxpayers. Among them were the Jarvisses.

The first is a very indistinct and dubious John in 1485. Where had he come from? It's probably now impossible to tell. Gervys is a fairly common name, particularly in East Anglia, and there had been some in Essex records for many years. But it may be that he had come from the Suffolk borders where there were Jarvisses around Clare, from which the original lords of Thaxted manor had taken their name, or even from London itself.

John Jarvis's sons seem to have included a William and a Thomas as these two paid tax on their goods in 1524, when Wolsey managed to persuade an unwilling Parliament to vote a subsidy for the new French war. The parish registers, although some of the earliest in the country, don't begin until 1538 when

Thomas Cromwell decreed that they should, and even so the earliest entries give only names with no descriptions to help put their owners in place. Is the William Jarvis who was buried in 1544 the father or the son of William Jarvis junior who paid his taxes that year along with Widow Jarvis, presumably his mother, and Thomas his brother, or is he the uncle? Where parents resolutely passed on their own names or those of the last generation to their children, there can only be deduction or guesswork.

Nor do I know any more about the jobs or homes of these first unquestionable ancestors of Samuel Jarvis or why they had come to Thaxted, though a later one described himself in his will as a weaver and perhaps it was the cloth trade that had brought them there. They were taxed only on their goods not on cattle like many of their neighbours and this suggests trade rather than agriculture.

The town itself has changed hardly at all in structure or in size of population since those days. It lies in the part of the county that is wooded and small-hilly unlike the flat lands near the sea. The main road from Great Dunmow and London leads uphill past the Guildhall to the church and the windmill at its top and then on towards Saffron Walden. By the sixteenth century the original manor house had long fallen into decay but 'old Cutte', as William Leland called him in his *Itinerary* written in Henry VIII's reign, 'builded Horeham-Haule, a very sumptuous house' with 'a goodly pond or lake by it and faire parkes thereabout' a couple of miles from the town when he was given the property in 1514. His rent for the manors was £57 . 7s and appropriately it was made part of the King's settlement in the doomed marriage treaty for Anne of Cleves. Cutt must have brought some trade to the district even in his rebuilding and provisioning, and work for local labour, as well as taking his position as lord of the manors of Thaxted, Horham and Spencers Fee very seriously. He enjoyed it for only six years but it passed to his son, grandson and great grandson, all of whom were named John after him.

The period at which the first public appearances of Jarvis in Thaxted was made is a hard one to grasp, a pause between the end of decades of war and the upheaval of the Reformation. It was still a united Christian world under the Pope but the writing was literally there for anyone to read.

22

Alas what shall we friars do
Now laymen know Holy Writ?
All about wherever I go
They confront me with it.

I think the devil brought it about
To write the Gospel in English
For wicked men are now so stout
They give us neither flesh nor fish.

If I say it is not fit
For priests to work wherever they go
They quote in answer Holy Writ
And say that Saint Paul did so.

Then they look on my habit
And say, 'Forsooth upon our oaths
Whether it is grey, black or white
It is worth all our wearing clothes.'

I say I beg not for me
But for them that have none.
They say, 'You have two or three
Give them that need thereof one.'

Thus our deceits are aspied
In this way and many more.
Few men bid us abide
But hurry us fast through the door.

Anticlericalism had a long tradition in England but this has a
new edge to it. It isn't the wickedness of the friar which is called
in doubt here, like the lascivious priest Jankin of an earlier poem,
but the whole premise on which he is set aside from other men.
As trade increased so too did literacy among those who needed it
for their expanding business, and once having learned to read
they might turn to illegal copies of the Bible. The ground was
being unconsciously prepared for the Reformation.

Essex before the migrations of the nineteenth century had a
long history of political and religious non-conformity and I should

like to think of William and Thomas Jarvis learning to read their samizdat scriptures but I can find no evidence for it and, unless the art was lost by their children or unless they could read without being able to write, they were, like so many of their descendants, illiterate, since their children sealed their wills with a mark even when bequeathing quite substantial property.

However, literacy and numeracy are not necessarily complementary and I think it likely that as thrifty yeomen they could count, certainly enough to make sure they were not cheated by tax farmer or bailiff. This was the heyday of the yeomen who were to be later romanticized by Shakespeare as the victors of Agincourt. Even Robin Hood in a fifteenth-century ballad was not an outlawed young nobleman, as he appears in some versions of the story, but a 'good yeoman', pledged to do no harm to the husbandman 'that tilleth his plough', and he charged Sir Richard of the Lee for the dinner he gave him in the greenwood, on the grounds that it had never been the custom for a yeoman to pay for a knight. In a society of warring nobles it was money, men thought, that would give a new security.

> Man on the earth whatsoever thou be
> I warn plainly thou getst no degree
> Nor will any worship abide with thee
> Unless thou have ready money to offer.

> If thou be a yeoman and a gentleman would be
> Into some lord's court put thou thee,
> Be sure thou have spending large and plenty
> And always ready money to offer.

The Jarvis women first make their public appearance by name in the parish registers. Lucy was buried in 1544 but whether she was maid, wife or widow the record doesn't say. In 1551 Margaret Reignold became a Jarvis when she married Thomas, only to die six weeks later in an epidemic known as 'the sweating sickness' which swept away thousands, including the two Brandons, sons of the Duke of Suffolk, within the same half hour. Brought up with the heir to the throne, the young Prince Edward, and mourned as two of the finest flowers cut down, they were sixteen and thirteen and renowned for their learning; the fever seems to have exercised some malign will in favour of the young. Eleven people were buried in Thaxted within three days in July.

The records don't show when Margaret's husband married again. He was the son of another Thomas Jarvis who was witness to a deed of sale in 1539. Probably he was himself the son of the Thomas who had paid his tax, along with William and Widow Jarvis for the French wars, unless indeed he was the same Thomas and lived to a very great age, for he didn't die until 1590.

He had married an Agnes who bore him several sons: Thomas, of course, William, James and John, the first three of whom died before their parents. In a deed conveying two and a half acres of land to his son James, Thomas is the first of the family to be described as 'yeoman', a status difficult to define. Bishop Hugh Latimer said of his own father that he was 'a yeoman, and had no lands of his own; only he had a farm of three or four pounds by the year at the uttermost, and hereupon he tilled so much as kept half a dozen men. He had walk for a hundred sheep, and my mother milked thirty kine; he was able and did find the King a harness with himself and his horse while he came to the place that he should receive the King's wages. I can remember that I buckled his harness when he went to Blackheath Field. He kept me to school: he married my sisters with five pounds apiece, so that he brought them up in godliness and fear of God. He kept hospitality for his poor neighbours, and some alms he gave to the poor and all this he did of the same farm, where he that now hath it payeth sixteen pounds by year or more, and is not able to do anything for his prince, for himself, nor for his children, or give a cup of drink to the poor'.

The Jarvisses could allege no such decline in their standard of living during the lifetime of Thomas, which coincided with one of the greater upheavals in British history, known since as the English Reformation. How the family responded to the religious changes can only be guessed at from the negative evidence: that they weren't prosecuted in either Catholic or Protestant reigns and they prospered. But either their position was not as high socially or as financially secure as that of Latimer's father or else, unlike him, they didn't have the ambition or imagination to send a son to school and then to nearby Cambridge, unless he was the Thomas who died outside the parish in 1559 and was brought home to be buried, Margaret's sometime husband.

James remained a husbandman; William's position is unknown.

John, though at first a husbandman, would probably later have described himself as yeoman too, since he seems to have inherited his father's 'now mansion house' when Thomas died. It looks as if William, who was labelled 'junior' in 1544, died childless in 1560 for an appropriately named burial appears then and Thomas Jarvis is the only one called on for tax in later returns.

So far the lives of the family are fairly clear but this genealogically tidy picture leaves out the David line. David Jarvis is the first entry of any Jarvis in the registers. He dies in 1540. Thereafter another in 1551, who is presumably his son, marries Emme Pers and they have David in 1559 and Alice in the following year. Emme dies in 1568 and David, 'senex' as the registers call him, in 1579, leaving a will. He has probably already, as the custom was, made provision for his son and so he leaves his remaining property to his daughter. He too describes himself as 'yeoman'.

'First I bequeath my soul to Almighty God my creator and my body to the earth to be buried within the churchyard of Thaxted aforesaid. Imprimis I give and bequeath unto the poor of Thaxted twelve pence to be distributed by the churchwardens . . . upon whom of the said poor they shall deem it most necessary and needful. Item I give and bequeath unto Alice Gervase my daughter all the whole use and occupying of that my house situated in a street called Newbiggen together with all such grounds as unto the same do appertain to be to the use and occupying of my said daughter and her assigns during the term of the said lease in as ample manner and form as I myself at the time of making this present testament by virtue of one lease from Robert Poole yeoman unto me made do hold and enjoy the same. Item I further give and bequeath unto my said daughter all and singular other goods and chattels whatsoever as well as moveables and unmoveables (my debts being paid and my funeral charges being discharged) together with all such debts and duties as unto me at this present in my wise are due . . .'

Alice is also made his sole executor and his neighbour, Edward Robinson, is the supervisor. 'In witness whereof I have hereunto subscribed my usual mark with mine own hand in the presence of Thomas Hallidaye, vicar of Thaxtead, the writer hereof . . .'

Robert Poole, who had sold David Jarvis the lease of his Newbiggen house, lived at the hamlet of Stanbrook outside the town, and was fellow witness with Thomas Jarvis there to the 1539 deed. His lands lay next to the two and a half acres Thomas granted to his son James in 1569, all of which in such a small town makes it almost certain that David was related to the other Jarvisses, perhaps another son of the first William.

His property was in the centre of town, near the church and the houses of his son David, who by the time of his death in 1608 had moved to the neighbouring village of Stebbing with his wife, Priscilla, who died four years later and to whom David left his Thaxted property, which included two houses in Townstreet and a house and garden in Fishrow. Their only child was a daughter who had married a William Bredge. By the paternalistic laws of genealogy this branch of the Jarvisses dies out of the family tree but it's interesting that David had been described in his will as a weaver and had been able to amass so much property in Thaxted before moving out to Stebbing. Alice, his sister, may be the one who married Daniel Hubby the year after her father's death or the one who died, still a spinster, six years later and was buried in Thaxted.

Marriages were, of course, arranged, not simply left to the desires of those most concerned, and parents were expected to provide some form of dowry for their daughters, even if only a few pounds from a yeoman father of the bride. Women could inherit and leave property, as Priscilla Jarvis did to her Bredge grandchildren, but if they were married anything they inherited became their husband's, so most female wills of the period are by widows. Where elaborate arrangements were necessary among wealthier families a marriage contract was drawn up showing what the wife's father and her husband had each agreed to. Among poorer families the impulse from the girl's relations must have been to protect her and her children in case of the husband's death or failure rather than a desire to add to their own wealth and prestige by a marriage alliance. In this light the dowry, which seems to modern eyes a slave-price, can be seen as a form of protection for a non-employed woman who would be too busy as a rule with the domestic economy and bearing children to make any money on her own behalf even had the law allowed her to keep it. There were at least two Jarvis girls who married for love before it was the norm but I shall come to them in their time.

The consumer society, is no modern invention. The greater part of our lives is spent, and has been for centuries, on the pursuit of simple needs and pleasures which we share with other animals: food, warmth, comfort and, because we are naked beasts, some form of adornment other than the utilitarian which will be the equivalent of the peacock's tail or the female chimpanzee's glowing pink behind. Because we are human we either make elaborate structures to satisfy these needs or disguise them from ourselves by inventing ideologies which try to discount them in favour of elaborated ideals, even sometimes trying to persuade ourselves that there was some period in human history when our consumer satisfactions didn't have to be met.

The will that Thomas Jarvis, the elder, made in 1588 two years before he died, and the year of the Armada, gives a picture of a way of country life that was hardly to alter for people of his class for another hundred years or more and must, to judge by earlier wills and letters, have been already in existence at least since the dying away of feudalism and the greater spread through the population of what are so rightly called 'creature comforts'. Not all his possessions are detailed, just those he wished to leave away from his remaining son John, who would inherit his father's house and its contents. However, because of the old man's affection for his granddaughter-in-law, Helen, the list is, conveniently, long enough to show how the sixteenth-century Jarvisses lived.

He begins with one round table and one cupboard from the hall of 'my now mansion house' and two joined buffet stools. These more elaborate forms of furniture, where the legs are joined by a crossbar, which enables the legs to be slimmer and more elegant while keeping the piece strong, are always specified and the unjoined were clearly thought to be cheaper, perhaps more rustic, articles. 'Buffet stools' were low, like footstools.

Next he deals with utensils: one great kettle, one cauldron, one brass pot, one quern to grind malt in, one latten mortar, one chafing dish, one latten ball candlestick, six pewter platters, one pewter basin and one pewter pot. 'Latten' was a species of brass alloy usually hammered into thin sheets for plating. A chafing dish held burning fuel to keep food hot on or even to cook it on as a kind of portable grate. The great kettle may actually be a grate kettle. He has bequeathed her the means to make food and drink, to keep it hot, dishes to put it in, plates to eat it off and light by which to see what you're eating. The modern dinner party needs no more. The malt is for the monthly brew of beer which was the staple drink from breakfast through the day.

After food comes sleep: 'one standing bedstead standing in the parlour, one feather bed, a bolster, two pillows, two blankets, one coverlet, one pair of towen sheets and a further four pairs of sheets, of which two are of flax and two are of tow.' There is more for the bedroom to come: 'one bedstead standing in the chamber over the hall of my house,' one mattress, one blanket, one bolster, one coverlet.

Helen hasn't quite finished. She is also to have two joined hutches, one powdering trough, one great tub or yielding vat, one little tub, three cream bowls and one bearing sheet. 'Hutches' were chests or coffers for keeping things in. Most of the other things belong to the wife's domain of the dairy. Hugh Latimer spoke of his mother as keeping the kine while his father walked the sheep. The vital powdering trough is for salting meat to see the household through the winter. The bearing sheet is a bit puzzling. It has to do with childbirth; a 'bearing cloth' could be a child's christening robe and the sheet is for carrying the baby to church in.

'Item I give unto the said Helen one flaxen boardcloth, one long towel and one short.' So ends Helen's share of the moveables which are valued at twenty shillings which her husband Thomas, 'the son of Thomas, my son deceased' is to pay to his cousin Thomas, 'the son of John my son,' but there still remain a one-leaved table standing in the hall and a cupboard in the buttery to go to Thomas, 'the son of James, my son deceased'.

The tablecloth and towels are touches of almost luxury, though the towels may be for use with the tablecloth rather than for drying after a wash. It is the comprehensiveness of these household goods that I find so impressive. They conjure up with their domestic solidity a series of pictures of that way of life like the illustrations to some book of hours.

Thomas Jarvis, the elder, yeoman also left a bullock to Helen; two milk cows and all his corn and grain to her husband Thomas; a little black ambling nag to James, son of James, and a brindled cow to his 'son-in-law', an ambiguous term that included stepson, William Overall. To the poor of Thaxted he gave 6s . 8d to be distributed on the day of his funeral. Was he so much richer than

David Jarvis, who died ten years before leaving twelve pence to the poor, or more generous or superstitious or merely the victim of inflation?

He has incidentally in the course of his will given us some useful details about the size and layout of his 'mansion house' which are also standard for a couple of hundred years for men of his status. There is the hall with the chamber above it, the parlour and the buttery. Meals were eaten in the hall, with any employed workpeople sitting down with the family. The parlour was the family bedroom; food and drink were kept in the buttery and possibly prepared there. The extra storey of the room over the chamber is an improvement on the older one-decker houses and was to spread over the remaining rooms in the coming decades.

Thomas and Helen had only been married just over two years when their grandfather made his will. To judge by the amount he gave them, they seemed to have been able to provide little for themselves. The girl was expected to spin and weave her own linen or else to bring it with her on her marriage, and to supply much of the household goods. Helen seems to have been curiously improvident. Thomas was made the old man's executor and the couple appear to be his favourites among his grandchildren. I feel that Helen, perhaps because of her name, must have charmed him and I wonder if the others watched her progress into his affections with envy, as still happens in similar family situations, while he prepared to leave her what Agnes, his wife, had brought him.

This kind of furnishing Shakespeare didn't think impossible for the Capulets' house.

1 Serv   Where's Potper, that he helps not to take away? He shift a trencher? He scrape a trencher!

2 Serv   When good manners shall lie all in one or two men's hands, and they unwash'd too, 'tis a foul thing.

1 Serv   Away with the join stools, remove the court cubbert, look to the plate. Good thou, save me a piece of marchpane . . .

Later old Capulet tells the servants to turn up the tables in the hall to make more room for dancing, to bring more light and damp down the fire because it has made the room too hot. The all-purposeness of the hall is very clear. Perhaps Helen danced in old Thomas Jarvis's much smaller hall and set the tongues wagging. Perhaps he was just such an old man as Capulet senior with one eye for the girls and memories of his youth.

> I have seen the day
> That I have worn a visor and could tell
> A whispering tale in a fair lady's ear . . .

Agnes, Thomas's wife, had died the year before. An Agnes who must be his granddaughter married in the year he made his will, and his son James had a daughter Agnes, as did Thomas's son John, though his Agnes had died in 1575. John is a shadowy figure. He had married Elizabeth Maskoll in 1559. They had had several children most of whom had died except for Thomas and Agnes and perhaps another John. When Elizabeth died in 1602 John married, six months later, a woman with the curious name of Wibora Bacon. I have seen her Christian name elsewhere among Essex records. It looks like a version of the very obscure St Wiborada of St Gall who has somehow found her way to East Anglia, compounded with a Saxon girl called rather improbably Wisburgh, war-fortress, who must be a sister of Brunhilda.

I have jumped ahead to the end of the century and must now go back to earlier happenings. Alice was the commonest name for Jarvis women at the beginning of the records, closely followed by Agnes. Alice had become popular because of the heroine of the French romance: Bel Alys. In 1551 Alice Jarvis married Robert Parker, the vicar of Little Bardfield. She was probably the sister of the David Jarvis who also married that year. Perhaps her mother's name was Alice.

Robert Parker had been to Cambridge University. He could of course read and write though it's very unlikely that his wife could: her will was dictated. A suitable candidate took his B.A. in 1512-13 and his M.A. three years later. By the time he married Alice Jarvis he was sixty-three, if the account of his age, ninety-five at his death, can be trusted. However, he was a spirited cleric and their first child was born the year of their marriage.

The parish is only three miles from Thaxted, with a small brick church and a population of a few hundred which has probably altered very little in size since then. Obviously it wasn't an appointment for anyone who was hoping to advance in the church and certainly not for someone in his sixties as Robert

31

Parker was at the time of his appointment and his marriage to Alice. Perhaps he had been married before or perhaps he was only now taking advantage of the increasing Protestantism of Edward's reign that made it permissible for the clergy to marry.

Robert was only just in time, for Edward VI died in 1553 and Mary tried to put the clock back so that he would have lost either his wife or his job. The parish registers describe him as rector and, at the burial of a son Robert in Thaxted during Mary's reign, as sacerdotus. It's extremely unlikely that Alice Jarvis would have married him against her family's wishes and I therefore conclude that they were Protestant enough to approve of her marrying a priest.

Socially as well as culturally there must have been some discrepancy between the families though many of the Essex clergy were notoriously poor and insufficiently educated for their jobs. It's frustrating not to know precisely who Alice's parents were though there may be something in the fact that her first child was called by that inevitable Jarvis Christian name: Thomas. Their other sons have the same names as those of Robert's contemporary, Matthew Parker, Archbishop of Canterbury. Clergy were of course often drawn from among the yeoman class, but this marriage is the only indication that the Jarvisses had any aspirations or contacts beyond the local and rural. It may simply be that Robert Parker at sixty-three wanted a healthy young wife of good country stock as a foil to himself. She certainly looked after him well, thereby fully justifying the wisdom of his choice.

Alice Jarvis's life was shaped in its most important aspect, the person she was to live with for nearly thirty years, by Erasmus and King Henry VIII. Without them and all that they jointly embodied of the new learning coupled with the political and personal desires of the King she would never have become a vicar's wife and moved into a different kind of society, for however countrified the priest, however much time he might spend on his own lands and animals, nevertheless he had to give a part of his life to reading, preaching, visiting and offering spiritual help and taking part in the imagery and poetry of the prescribed services. Robert Parker must have supplemented his income from tithes and benefactions by agriculture, much as Ralph Joslin, the vicar of Earles Colne fifteen miles away, found he still had to do a hundred years later, spending in the end perhaps more thought on his farm than on his cure of souls.

Essex had for long been a notoriously radical county in matters of religion, dominated as it was intellectually by the closeness of Cambridge. John Ball, who was instrumental in Wat Tyler's 1381 rising, was a preacher at Colchester and beliefs dating from then had never entirely died out in the area, though of necessity they had gone underground. They were given a fresh upsurge as the new learning of Erasmus, More and Colet percolated through society becoming more practically revolutionary as it went. The King's need for a divorce provided the legal climate for those ideas to grow and Essex people were quick to respond.

Thaxted had its own local monastery to be dissolved as part of the process. Tilty Abbey was only a couple of miles from the town and was part of the old Clare holdings. For many years there had been conflict between the town and the abbey because the town had to pay the monks a tithe. This seems to have been reduced about the time that the parish church was built in Thaxted but the abbey still owned property in the area. Its generally admitted unsatisfactory abbot, Roger, was summoned with other monastic heads to give an account of Tilty before Convocation at Canterbury in 1529. Shortly after, he was replaced by John Palmer, but nothing could stop the suppression and in February 1535 Tilty was handed over to Richard Cromwell by the abbot and five others who seemed to be the entire complement, at least one of whom was in fairly regular correspondence with Thomas Cromwell.

A year later Richard Cromwell was paid £4 . 8s . 4d for his expenses in the suppression and in 1537 the roof lead was melted into 'sows' and sold. The abbot and the brothers, his mother and two dependants, 'impotent persons', together with five servants, were allowed to stay on 'till the King's further pleasure'. The inventory, apart from a rich selection of altar cloths, two 'of white Bruges satin with spots like drops of blood, of red velvet', and vestments, 'a cope of Turkey red satin and white lawnd wrought with gold, a cope of blue damask and three of silk branched and wrought with beasts of gold', and some silver plate, which was delivered to Richard Cromwell reads very like the household moveables of Thomas Jarvis with brass pots, kettles, feather bed, latten candlesticks, pewter plates and brewing vats. There was more of everything for a larger household of course, but the main differences are in the hangings of mixed silk and wool or painted cloth and the carpets, surprisingly to us, to cover the table, cupboard and sideboard. The Marchioness of Dorset remained in residence throughout the suppression besieging Thomas Cromwell with begging letters on behalf of herself and various indigent relatives.

Much is made of the loss to the poor by the takeover of the monasteries, in terms of relief, medical aid and education, but in the case of Thaxted it has to be said that all these were more effectively provided by the secular charities attached to the parish church and administered by the churchwardens, in particular Yardleys' charity, which maintained the almshouses and their inhabitants. Sir Thomas Audley, writing to Cromwell in 1538 to try to save St John's, Colchester, and St Osyth's by converting them into colleges speaks of: 'Colchester wherein dwell many poor people which have daily relief of the house; another cause both these houses be in the end of the shire of Essex where litel hospitality shall be kept if these be dissolved . . . There is also twentie houses gret and smal dissolved in the shire of Essex already.' However, he was not averse to the Audley family acquiring the buildings and some of the rents of Tilty in 1542 after the death of the Marchioness of Dorset who had been given a sixty-year lease on them by the King.

The Tilty properties were far flung and a great many people managed to get a piece of them either as a freehold or a tenancy. The Duke of Suffolk got a farm in Thaxted 'called Venors alias Venouris' which had been held by Robert Poole, the Jarvisses' neighbour, which the Duke alienated to John and Agnes Wiseman. This farm has caused some difficulty to historians. The most famous of them, Morant, writing in 1764 listed it as an old manor of Thaxted, and it has been derived from a Norman family, but it seems to me more likely that the name is a corruption of Fenn, a family which in various spellings had been in the district for hundreds of years already. Some of them at least were cutlers but they also owned land. In 1577 James Jarvis had 'a parcel of landes late Fann's in the lane', and the same year John Jarvis stood surety with her father-in-law for the appearance at Chelmsford Assize of Margaret Fann, wife of John junior, on an unspecified charge. Five years later a John Fann married

Elizabeth Jarvis.

The Jarvis properties lay mostly between Monk Street, Tilty and Chickney in the manor of Horam Hall. Thomas Jarvis took part in a court baron there in 1555 and again in 1561 and 1569. No doubt he made his appearances to do his duty on the manorial jury, known as the homage, in other years too but the records are incomplete. Once he gave apologies for absence for Richard Purcas, for tenants were obliged to be present at these courts and were fined as defaulters unless excused according to the proper form. The list of defaulters appears at the end of the account of the day's business and a Jarvis often figures among them. Some of them were people who still owned leases of manor properties which they had sublet while living elsewhere themselves.

The tenants at Thaxted contributed twenty pence a head to the lord for the expenses of the court. They chose the constables and those who were to oversee the quality and measurement of bread and ale. Then they got down to cases and to noting changes in tenancy. The cases were such that still arise between neighbours: whose overflow is damaging someone else's property, who has cut down trees without permission or allowed his fences and hedges to decay so that his animals trample someone else's fields, who isn't doing his share in the common parts.

Exercising his duty in suit of court, as it was known, gave a man more of an investment in his community, a knowledge of simple law, a chance to meet others and discuss national and local events at dinner in one of the many Thaxted inns afterwards. It gave him an involvement in local politics which trained him for a wider exercise when summoned for jury service at assize or quarter sessions or to vote for the knight of the shire in national elections. It made too for a less docile rural population in both politics and religion. In 1544 Robert Ward of Thaxted was made to recant for expounding the Scriptures in alehouses, 'chiefly when taken with ale', keeping unlawful books and leading others into like folly. He is a forerunner of a line of pub-politicians.

And now my song is ended and I hope you'll all agree
If you want any pointers, well you'd better send for me.
But I warn you I'm not worth a damn till I empty two or three
Of the very biggest tankards in the public bar.

But some of the manifestations of disaffection were more serious. In 1549 women and boys broke down the fences of some of the new owners of monastic lands, who had enclosed them as part of the growing concentration on sheep farming, and again in 1577 the women, this time of Brentwood, took over a chapel that the owner was trying to withold from them in order to pull it down. Seditious bills and writings were found on various occasions, and on the death of Edward VI the county was divided between the supporters of Mary and those of Lady Jane Grey, whose leader lost his head on Tower Hill. Not surprisingly, radical Protestant Essex seethed with sedition during the reign of Mary, and eleven men and two women were burned together on Stratford Green, but even Elizabeth didn't escape entirely from slanderous rhymers and 'lewd and inconvenient speeches'.

Besides the training in rudimentary law and its exercise, the manor courts were valuable in regulating relationships between neighbours and defusing many potentially litigious or dangerous situations. As long as the participants didn't become divided into factions there were advantages in having local questions decided by local people who understood both the characters of the persons involved and the implications of a problem. 'John Jarvis is to dig and cleanse the ditch that abuts onto the land of John Hall at the Stanbrook before the feast of the Purification of the Blessed Virgin Mary on pain of a fine.' Neighbours would know the lie of the ground, that the obligation to maintain that ditch had always gone with that piece of property and that if it wasn't done the Stanbrook would flood the wretched Hall's parcel of land.

In 1578 the queen herself came to stay at Horam Hall with the then Sir John Cutt. It is probable though not entirely certain that she stayed on other occasions too. A letter from 'the court at Horam' from Lord Burghley suggests that she was there in 1571 but the 1578 visit is indisputably recorded in the Acts of the Privy Council which sat, on this occasion at least, in Thaxted. Unfortunately the churchwardens' accounts that must have included the ringing of the bells, even if nothing more elaborate, to celebrate her entry to the town are missing, but it seems only reasonable to suppose that the whole population would have turned out, the mayor and local gentry to present formal welcomes and compliments and perhaps a gift, the boys of the grammar school, with their headmaster, to make the inevitable Latin speech, and the rest of the inhabitants to fill in the background with cheers and infants thrust forward for Elizabeth's blessing in return for a nosegay. Among them would surely have been the Jarvisses, Thomas and his progeny and perhaps David and Priscilla, ridden over from Stebbing for the event.

> No sooner was pronounced the name
>> but babes in street gan leap;
> The youth, the age, the rich, the poor,
>> came running all on heap,
> And clapping hands, cried mainly out,
>> 'O blessed be the hour!
> Our Queen is coming to the Town,
>> with princely train and power.'

The royal procession would have itself been worth it even if there were no fair or other celebration. The Earls of Warwick and Leicester were both in attendance as well as Lord Burghley and the officers of the royal household, Mr Comptroller, Mr Vicechamberlain, the beautiful Sir Christopher Hatton, nicknamed 'Legs' by the Queen, Mr Treasurer and Mr Secretary Wilson. The Queen stayed at Horham Hall for at least a week but there is unfortunately no record of her entertainment there, whether there was dancing and music or a play to pass the September days, apart from the two privy council meetings. She would bring all her own furnishings and provide the cost of the food, but those who entertained her were often out of pocket and perhaps her visits contributed to the financial straits of later members of the Cutt family. Sir John seems to have been quite a favourite for on one occasion when there was plague in London she sent him the Spanish ambassador who professed to be offended by the shortness of his name. The food bill still exists for her visit to nearby Ingatestone Hall in 1561 for only four days: beer by the tun of course, some Shakespearean samphire, olives and capers, 5 gallons of cream, 693 eggs, comfits, sugar, cloves, fruit, including 12 pound of prunes, and a massacre of wild and tame fowl, bitterns, shoveller ducks, egrets, pewits, cygnets, quails, herons, domestic pullets, geese.

The streets of Thaxted would have been cleaned and decorated for the visit. It was usual for a town to offer a silver gilt cup but there's no record of whether Thaxted managed to rise to this. The queen herself rode on horseback or in an open litter so that everyone could see her.

O come again, sweet beauty's sun:
When thou art gone, our joys are done.

Old David Jarvis might have been able to join the watching crowd, perhaps leaning on his daughter Alice's shoulder, and I feel that Thomas the patriarch would have made it somehow, helped by his sons William and John and their wives and children. But the conspicuously missing figure would have been Thomas's son James who had died two years before, closely followed by his nine-year-old son Robert, to whom as the eldest of his children he had left the lease of his tenement and forty acres which he had bought from Sir John Cutt in 1574. It would not have surprised James to know that young Robert would follow him quickly to the grave for James believed himself to have been bewitched.

1st witch	Where hast thou been sister?
2nd witch	Killing swine.
3rd witch	Sister where thou?
1st witch	A sailor's wife had chestnuts in her lap

And munch'd, and munch'd, and munch'd:-
   "Give me,"
quoth I:
"Aroint thee, witch!" the rump-fed ronyon cries.
Her husband's to Aleppo gone, master o' the Tiger:
But in a sieve I'll thither sail,
And like a rat without a tail,
I'll do, I'll do, and I'll do . . .
I will drain him dry as hay:
Sleep shall neither night nor day
Hang upon his penthouse lid;
He shall live a man forbid:
Weary se'nnights nine times nine
Shall he dwindle, peak, and pine.

By general consent Essex was a 'bad country, I think even one of the worst in England' for witchcraft. 'They say there is scarce any town or village in all this shire, but there is one or two witches at least in it,' George Gifford, a contemporary writer, and Essex vicar, made a character say in one of his dialogues on the subject. The underlying web of superstition from which such beliefs might arise certainly persisted in Essex until the late nineteenth century for Samuel or Lydia took it with them when they moved to London and it was passed on down to their grandchildren and even great-grandchildren although by then it had become more a quaint ritual than anything to be seriously believed. Most of it consisted of simple charms to ward off ill luck or purchase good. For some misfortunes, breaking a mirror, having a picture fall from the wall or a bird fly into the house or seeing the new moon through glass, there was nothing to be done. But for seeing the tail of a white horse or disinfecting any malign influence from a coin or a lump of coal picked up in the street and to be brought home, spit was the sovereign cure. To make the new moon beneficent, you bowed three times and turned your silver coins over.

An itching palm meant money coming if it was the right hand and going if it was the left. An itching foot meant travel. Dropped cutlery foretold the sex and age of visitors. A variety of signs told of letters: from falling coals in the grate to froth on the tea. Green for clothes or furnishings always brought disaster and so did many flowers if admitted to the house. As children we believed in witches and ghosts, as Reginald Scot noted in *The Discoverie of Witchcraft* in 1584 children are prone to do, but in Essex itself a supposed witch was badly mobbed as late as the mid-nineteenth century not by children but by adults. Maud on one of her childhood visits to Granny's saw a bent old woman in black come out of the almshouses and thought she was a witch.

James Jarvis's witch was Alice Hinxson, widow. On the 20th of January 1572 she bewitched three cows of his worth £4 and seven ewes worth twenty shillings 'by reason of which they died within four days'. She was tried, found guilty and sentenced to be pilloried four times and serve a year in gaol. None of the depositions of witnesses survive to fill out the details of the case but from the many others which follow a similar pattern it's possible to surmise that she had come begging for something, a little milk, money or meat, and been refused. These were the commonest beginnings of such episodes. The witch goes away muttering and misfortune follows.

There had been another witch at work in Thaxted the same year, Elizabeth Taylor, wife of John, a labourer: 'a common witch and enchantress', who bewitched the daughter of a carpenter to death and followed this up with a similar curse on the daughter of a London carpenter the following year. She was tried at the same assize at Brentwood as James Jarvis's Alice Hinxson. She too was found guilty but she was sentenced to be hanged. Only encompassing a human death by witchcraft brought the capital penalty. Alice Hinxson's was the standard sentence laid down for lesser offences. Once a quarter she was 'in some market town upon the market day or such time as any fair be kept there to stand openly upon the pillory by the space of six hours and there shall openly confess her error and offence'.

Alice didn't live to fulfil this. She died in Colchester gaol of plague, or 'divine visitation' as the coroners called it in such cases, in 1575. Hers was the last prosecution that has survived from Thaxted for another fifteen years when Margaret Snell was found guilty of bewitching a woman to death. After that there is only George Taylor, Thaxted's cunning man or white witch, who was resorted to from all over the county by people who had lost things and was accused of 'thereby deceiving divers people'. Aside from him, there were therefore only three cases, or four if Elizabeth Taylor's two are taken separately, in Thaxted in a period of 150 years which saw over 470 indictments in Essex, which actually outnumber those for the other four counties of the Home Circuit put together. The eighty-two executions alone are well over double those for all the rest.

Compared with Stebbing, to which David Jarvis junior had moved and which had a much smaller population but half a dozen prosecutions, Thaxted's figures are mild. Some villages seem to have been victims of mass hysteria like that which infected American Salem. Others were undoubtedly affected by stories of what had happened elsewhere since news of white witches, who were often resorted to to lift the curse of a black witch, travelled throughout the county. But some villages, including Robert Parker's Little Bardfield, had seemingly no witches at all, even when they were next door to one which produced several.

Thaxted's record, then, for a population of roughly two thousand was quite good. Why therefore did James Jarvis become involved? There have been many attempts to explain the witch scare and in particular its extreme manifestation in Essex. Some writers have put it down to religious changes and the breakdown of the accepted social obligation of charity. It's probably true that indigent old women were among some of the most frequent customers of the monastic charities and that without this source of help they would be thrown back on neighbours or the parish. In this explanation James Jarvis feels guilty for refusing help to Widow Hinxson and expresses his guilt by accusing her of witchcraft.

Another hypothesis is that witchcraft is a way of accounting for otherwise inexplicable misfortune. In this context Essex's Protestantism, already verging on Puritan Non-conformity, is worth considering. According to the views expressed by George Gifford, vicar of Maldon, in his treatise on witchcraft in the county, misfortune is a visitation from God. 'These things are sent to try us.' This, although theologically consistent, needs a strong and indeed a logical mind to accept. We must believe either that our loving father god is punishing us, in which case we must have sinned, or that he is testing our faith in him with afflictions, as he did Job's, and in both cases we must accept with humility and stand firm whatever happens. The alternative is to 'curse God and die'. Even if we argue that the witchcraft has really taken place, in Protestant terms this is because the devil is using the witch to do his work. However he is only allowed to do so because God permits him to try us in this way. To believe anything else is to doubt the omnipotence of God and to fall into the heresy of the Manichees, making the devil as powerful as God.

Obviously it was much easier both emotionally and intellectually for an illiterate farmer simply to fall back on the superstition that he was bewitched, to blame a malign old woman rather than himself for sin or God for punishing him or trying him. Yet even so this doesn't explain why it should be James Jarvis who was susceptible to this idea to the point that resulted in her death. Other people's cattle and children died all the time but not everyone looked for a witch as the instrument. Whatever the social and religious factors which provide the background for witchcraft beliefs, the ultimate explanation of why a particular person brings an accusation to the notice of the law when hundreds don't must lie in individual psychology.

The figure of the witch is heavily charged. It's no accident that, although men might be witches, by far the greater number, certainly in England, were women. Both Alice Hinxson and later Margaret Snell had no obvious relations in Thaxted that appear in the registers. There are no Snells at all and only two, much earlier, Hinxson burials but no christenings or marriages. This seems to establish that they were stereotype lonely old women. Elizabeth Taylor, although a married woman, also seems without local connections. Her husband John wasn't buried in the parish church, nor were they married there and there is no evidence of any children.

James Jarvis had married Catherine Pory in 1566. They had at least three children, Agnes, Robert and Thomas, before the bewitching and one after, James, before James senior died in 1578. There's no record of his wife's death or remarriage. Presumably she brought up the remaining children. Either James married late or he was still a young man when he died. If the latter it suggests — and the death of his son Robert at only nine perhaps reinforces this — that James wasn't physically strong, and perhaps at the time when he lost his cows and sheep he was struggling hard to reach the position he did two years later, when he was able to lease a house and forty acres from Sir John Cutt.

As well as this main property, he had also managed to buy nine acres in the old common field of Cursall, whose strips had been split and sold off, and another two pieces which he doesn't mention in his will but which also passed to his children. Sixty years later Alice Hinxson was still commemorated in 'a parcel of land called Witchcroft' for which Daniel Jarvis paid 6d rent.

The Jarvis houses stood less than a mile from Horham Hall. Perhaps the music for La Volta, the dance that the Queen was so fond of, penetrated the quiet woods as far as their lattice and horn windows, or one of the family, out on that favourite local sport, poaching in the park, got close enough to Horham's glazed windows to peer in. Even respectable yeomen appear frequently on a charge of night-walking and the Shakespeare legend of his poaching in Sir Thomas Lucy's park may well have more truth in it than has been supposed. However, if the Jarvisses did poach they were clever or lucky enough not to be caught.

What shall he have that hath slain the deer?
His leather coat and horns to wear.

About the time of the Queen's first visit to Horham, three Thaxted men, Thomas Stebbing, tanner, John Badcock, tailor, and John Hubbard, husbandman, took their black greyhound into the park at two in the morning to course a deer but were put out to find another party already at work. It was John Badcock's younger son Henry who later married Martha Jarvis, another daughter of Thomas. A piquant entry in the churchwarden's accounts lists payment to 'Goodman Badcocke for wine for the communion' and another to 'Huberd and Jervice for eight days work paving the church,' when they were all older and grown respectable.

In many ways, of course, Elizabeth herself was the greatest enchantress of them all and that was perhaps another reason why witchcraft seemed so rife in her reign. Another element might be a dislike of petticoat rule: if a queen might reign why not a wife or a mother? By law the wife was entitled to a third of the husband's goods and estate but James Jarvis made no such provision for Catherine whom he doesn't describe as 'my loving' or 'dear wife' as many testators do. Instead he merely gives her, as an afterthought towards the end of the will, the use of the small parcel of land intended for his two younger sons until they reach the age of twenty. It's true he makes her fellow executor with his brother William but this seems a cold formality, less care than he had shown for his daughter Agnes, to whom he left twenty marks, and it contrasts with the aged Robert Parker's concern for his Alice, leaving her his house in Thaxted for her convenience and ease.

A whiff of sadness comes somehow from James Jarvis across the centuries, compounded with the stink of Colchester gaol and the plaguey end of Alice Hinxson, widow. It's reassuring to know that in some places the voice of reason and commonsense was being raised and would eventually result in the end of the witchcraft trials although not before Matthew Hopkins, witch-finder general, had caused a new terror in Essex. 'One sort of such as are said to be witches,' wrote Reginald Scot in his famous treatise, 'are women which be commonly old, lame, bleare-eyed, pale, foul, and full of wrinkles . . . They are lean and deformed, shewing melancholy in their faces to the horror of all that see them. They are doting, scolds, mad, divilish . . . These miserable wretches are so odious unto all their neighbours, and so feared as few dare offend them or deny them anything they ask: whereby they take upon them; yea and sometimes think, that they can do such things as are beyond the ability of human nature.'

This must stand as the epitaph of Alice Hinxson.

III My *Will and Plain Meaning*

When Thomas Jarvis, the eldest, died in 1590, two years after making his will, the golden age of Elizabeth was over. In spite of the success against the Armada, the rest of the reign was to be full of alarms of invasion and foreign excursions. For the ambitious young men, like John Donne, who followed the Earl of Essex and Raleigh on their foreign expeditions, it was a time of pride and excitement after the sluggardliness of peace but to the pressed men and those whose taxes supplied the wars it was a time of anxiety and dearth made worse by a series of bad harvests in the late nineties.

One hundred and fifty men were pressed in Essex in 1591 as part of the expedition to Normandy to help the new protestant King of France, Henry of Navarre, gain his throne. The expedition was a success and Elizabeth was able later in the year to issue instructions about her soldiers' treatment on their return to civvy street, to their old employ and homes. The parishes were to relieve the wounded until they were able to work again. But many never came back. Their parcels of land fell to new tenants and the lords of the manor scooped up the fines due at the manor courts on the exchange of owners.

Meanwhile the muster master, Captain Peacock, who had 'greatly perfected and made more skilful' the Essex men before they set out, hadn't been paid by the county for his training. More men were needed the following year. Their coats were paid for at four shillings apiece and their conduct money to the port was eightpence a day for seven days for three hundred men, roughly the daily wage recommended under the Statute of Artificers and Labourers by the Essex Grand Jury in 1599.

Along with the levies of Middlesex and Buckinghamshire, the Essex men were specially praised for being 'hable and sufficient',

well armed, 'personable and soldierlike', to the great glory of
Queen and country. The abstaining from meat in Lent was
reinforced and one butcher was appointed in every town to
supply flesh for the sick and weak, the proceeds from the licences
to slaughter to go to maimed soldiers throughout the kingdom.
No doubt there were a few skivers to exploit such a situation as
there always are.

> To England will I steal, and there I'll steal;
> And patches will I get unto these cudgell'd scars,
> And swear I got them in the Gallia wars.

The family seem to have escaped all the levies. Thomas
Reynolds, Will Hubberd, Thomas Annys and Robert Taylor
were sent from Thaxted to the Low Countries in 1599. The next
year Edward Reeve and Edmond Fetch went to Ireland and in
1602 Christopher Wakeling, James Townsend and Thomas
Reynolds, who seems to have been something of a professional,
followed them. Two Jarvisses did get drafted from the county:
William from High Easter and Thomas from Laindon, either of
whom could be a relative of the Thaxted branch. There was also
a threat of a new Spanish invasion. The Essex coastal beacons
were manned and the trained bands mustered. All able-bodied
men were to attend with their own arms and armour. 1,150
'ablemen' were the usual number to turn out for Dunmow
Hundred, and among them several of the Jarvisses must have
assembled, like the Wessex militia Hardy described when the
danger was Napoleon, to drill and practise their arms.

All this cost money. Elizabeth had spent a great deal of her
own. Now she was forced to ask for a subsidy. With twenty-nine
of his neighbours, Thomas Jarvis paid twenty shillings' tax on his
lands. The invasion rumours grew. Provision was made for
powder and match, for dealing with those who spread false tales
and despondency, for impounding the horses of Catholics who
might support the enemy, for keeping the chief men of every
county at home to take part in the local defence.

Essex was slow to pay its share of the loan but these new
anxieties when the Spanish were actually in the Channel spurred
the money out of unwilling purses, helped by the improved
harvest of 1597 after three years when 'the green corn

> Hath rotted ere his youth attained a beard.'

Now it was the hoarders who kept up the prices, 'persons more like to wolves or cormorants than to natural men', men already rich whom 'the inferior sort grieved to see inrich by these ingrossings'. Orders were sent to the High Sheriff and the J. P.s of Essex to deal with the hoarders and those who kept the price of corn at an artificial level.

Thaxted had its own special excitements. The year after old Thomas Jarvis named Francis Rayner, yeoman, one of his executors, Rayner was summoned by the Privy Council to London about another will. Order was made for his keep during the case, which was eventually heard at Nonesuch. One Edward Hubberd had retained £100 due, under the will of his uncle Thomas Packsall of Thaxted, to be laid out in the founding of a free school at Stansted Montfichet, one of the many double-barrelled Essex villages. The hand of the government reached down even to the wills of ordinary men.

A few years later the Thaxted inhabitants petitioned Lord Burghley about the behaviour of John Wake, one of the Dunmow Hundred high constables 'who, if the information be true doth demean himself very badly in his office and is not meet to be continued therein'. Then in 1597 Thaxted had its own ring of counterfeiters: Robert Buck, William Lillie and one Sawyer, who were cutting fake seals and selling them for twenty shillings apiece.

The Jarvisses continued to lead, it seems, peaceful law-abiding lives. While their neighbours broke into and took over each other's homes, were hired to commit murder, rioted in Clavering, or forcibly expelled a woman from her pew in the parish church, they either remained quiet or weren't prosecuted. Whether they appeared before the Church courts accused of crimes against morality can't be known since the records have vanished. Thaxted only appears peripherally mentioned in outside cases, such as that of the woman being sued for breach of promise, who said that although the man had given her a silver whistle at Thaxted fair, it 'was a twelve month for a fairing but not for any respect of marriage'. Perhaps this was the fair held on the Sunday before Whitsun 'in like disorder' to others in the county.

Fairday was, as it was to remain in the country for the next three centuries, one of the chief opportunities for amusement. It therefore attracted the wrath of the godly, who claimed through the mouth of a Parson Harrison that the fairs had fallen from their original purpose and become 'paltry, little else bought or sold in them more than good drink, pies and some peddlery trash'. There had previously been a Corpus Christi play in Great Dunmow, which neighbouring parishes had attended and made collections for, a William Fann being one of the collectors in 1547. He was paid eightpence for two days 'gathering'. The play had gradually been supplanted by sports: archery with silver prizes, jumping and the more mysterious 'games of the Tavell' and 'games of our cunning'. By the church-wardens' accounts this was accompanied by much eating, drinking and dancing. Dunmow also had Christmas festivities, with a Lord of Misrule, and Mayday and Plough Feast celebrations. There were payments for brewing and baking, for pepper, saffron, honey, for looking after the horses, and to the minstrels, up to the end of Henry VIII's reign. It seems unlikely that all these activities stopped then although the mystery play itself was discontinued.

As well as these lawful amusements some of the male Jarvisses might have enjoyed illegal and riotous football, or the more peaceful though equally illegal, in spite of Sir Francis Drake, bowls or dice. For the women there was much less sport, apart from singing and dancing. Indeed sports in general were frowned upon unless, like archery, they could be useful to the state. Idleness was both a sin and a crime for the members of the lower classes who owned land worth less than forty shillings a year or goods worth less than ten pounds.

If they were craftsmen who had been brought up or worked in a list of specified trades, such as tailor, pewterer, butcher or arrowhead maker, and were unmarried men or women or married men under thirty, they could be compelled, if unemployed, to work for any master in their craft. If they had no trade, unemployed males between twelve and sixty could be compelled to take agricultural work, and two J.P.s could order any unmarried and unemployed woman between twelve and forty into menial service.

Working hours from mid-March to mid-September were from 5 a.m. to 7 or 8 p.m., fourteen or fifteen hours with two and a half allowed for meals, and dawn to dusk in the winter. Fortunately there were many Church festivals still, as well as the traditional fortnight off at Christmas. Wages were regulated and were either with or without 'meat and drink'. They varied between winter rates of 3d a day with subsistence, to 8d without, and 4d and 10d for the summer. The sixpence that Bottom's fellow actors hoped for from the Duke for him was roughly what he would have earned at his trade. Masters could be fined for paying more but also for undue dismissal.

The Thomas Jarvis who paid his twenty shillings tax for the French wars was more likely to be at risk as employer than worker. But which Thomas Jarvis was he? He was undoubtedly one of the three grandsons of old Thomas and most likely 'son of my son Thomas deceased' who had married Helen. Thomas, the son of John, seems to have married a girl called Ellinor while Thomas, the eldest surviving son of bewitched James, married Mary Neale in 1593. There were therefore three Thomas Jarvisses fathering children in the period from 1585-1615 and it is very hard to say which child belongs to which father, particularly since the registers don't give the names of the mothers which would have settled all the problems. Sometimes the registers merely record the name of the baby without that of either parent.

A rent roll for 1597 shows, among the twelve families living at Stanbrook and Hayway or Haggers, Thomas Jarvis senior, Thomas Jarvis junior and John Jarvis, while David Jarvis, the Stebbing weaver, has houses in Town Street and Fish Rowe, and another Thomas Jarvis had commuted the old manorial carriage service of four days' work to an annual rent of twenty-five shillings. There's no 'senior' or 'junior' beside this last Thomas so perhaps he is the third grandson of that name. Thomas Jarvis senior should be the son of Thomas, Thomas junior should be the son of James while Thomas, son of John, was still at home with his father. Another possibility for the Thomas who pays carriage rent is a new generation Thomas, son of Thomas and Helen.

The shadowy John Jarvis, old Thomas's remaining son, had had a son John in 1569, who married Philippa Stoner in 1592 and in his turn had a son John in 1597. The whole line of them passes through the registers like the pale ghosts who menaced Macbeth and leaves no imprint on history, local or family.

The Jarvis women continued to marry and bear children, and sometimes, outliving their husbands, to leave wills. Agnes, who married John Burton, left small sums to her children and grandchildren and 'to Richard my son all those goods of mine that he hath in his house except one press and that I give to the children of the said Richard except one flaxen sheet which I will be buried in'. Women were usually particular about bequeathing their clothes. The basic garments remained in fashion for many decades in rural society, though no doubt retouched with different ribbons and trimmings. Agnes gave 'my apparel to my good daughter-in-law Sysly Burton and her children'.

Alice Parker, the wife of the vicar of Little Bardfield, had quite a wardrobe to bequeath. Her son Robert was to have her best gown and her worst red petticoat, presumably not for his own use, and his daughter Elizabeth was to get 'my old black gown'. Son Mathew is to get his mother's best red petticoat and her best hat; her daughter-in-law Margaret is to get her best russet (grey) petticoat, a gorget and a pair of hose. Then there are gifts to women who may be servants: Annis Harrowed is to have an old gown, Mary Hawkesley is to have an old russet petticoat, a smock and an apron, Curty Smith, the midwife of Great Bardfield, is to have her best smock and Purkess's wife an old smock and an apron. John Thedon, a witness, is to have her best handkerchief and Mistress Joyce another handkerchief.

Alice Parker wasn't the only Alice Jarvis to marry into the clergy. Three years after her marriage another Alice from the same family, presumably her cousin, married William Huckle, brother or son of Thomas Huckle, the vicar of Gamlingay in Cambridge, and perhaps a relative of the Essex puritan divine John Huckle, who was driven to America by his refusal to conform. Alice's brother, William Jarvis, followed her to Gamlingay where he was said in the 1560s to be about thirty, free 'and has lived there six years, before that at Thaxted Essex from infancy of a Thaxted family'. These two look like children of William, old Thomas's brother. Did Robert Parker pass on to Thomas Huckle, fellow clerk, that Jarvis girls made good wives? If William was Thomas's son, Thomas must have been a strong Protestant who married before clerical marriages were officially allowed. There's no record of his taking a degree at either Oxford or, as might be expected, at Cambridge, the stronghold of the reformers.

In a society where marriages are arranged the partners are an added comment on the status of the family. The Jarvisses generally married yeomen or the children of yeomen from the roughly three hundred and fifty families of all kinds in the town. Sometimes Jarvis men married outside the borough. Philippa Stoner who married John seems to have no connection with Thaxted. Sometimes a Jarvis girl, like Alice who went to Gamlingay, must have married away but many of them stayed close to home and were linked with established Thaxted families: Fann, Andrewes, Neale, Crowe, Rolf and Hastler.

Mostly they pass their lives leaving records of children born, burials, children's marriages and little more. But sometimes the records have an addition that reveals a story, like the posthumous birth of Abigail Hastler to Ann, née Jarvis, after the death the year before of her exotically named husband Cesar.

Thomas and Helen, old Thomas's favourite grandchildren, had a son John, probably the son of Thomas born in 1594, whose marriage must have set the tongues wagging. In 1612 a Katherine Taylor married one John Ackworth who had been born, the son of John, in 1585. There are very few mentions of an Ackworth family in the registers. One, Francis, who had married Joan Onyon from one of the better-off Thaxted families, is described at his burial by a Latin word that means of either the seashore or river bank. It turns him into a character from *The Wind in the Willows*, a river-banker, and certainly suggests that he was thought of as rather an outsider.

Katherine Taylor, daughter of Richard, had been baptised in 1601. Now unless she was baptised some time after her birth, she must have been about twelve, the legal age of consent for girls, when she was married. Child brides weren't totally unknown at this time but they were uncommon, particularly in the lower classes. John Ackworth died after he had been married just over a year in November 1614. Fourteen months later Katherine had her baby son baptised John. Not surprisingly the vicar recorded the child as 'spurious' son of Katherine widow. Less than three months after its baptism Katherine married John Jarvis.

Her baby was the only bastard among the sixty baptisms in the register that year, though there were three the year following. It looks as if John Jarvis came calling on the young widow very soon after her husband's death and quickly bedded her.

For beauty and fine clothes
None could excel her.
She was proper stout and tall,
Her fingers long and small
She's a comely dame withal,
She's a brisk young widow.

A lover soon there came,
A brisk young farmer,
With his hat turned up all round
Thinking to gain her . . .

It was convenient that his name was John too.

The story of Katherine Taylor is the stuff of soap opera and perhaps helps to explain the perennial attraction of the form, whether in published fiction or on the television screen. She is the potential centrepiece of a Victorian partwork and her story could be adapted for *Coronation Street* with hardly a change: Katherine the girl who either couldn't wait to be married or was married off by her father, young, against her will and who was then seduced after her husband's death. A string of episodes could be taken up with the variations on her tale. And there are dozens of folk songs dramatizing different aspects of her story, from 'Mother I longs to be married', to 'I wish, I wish but it's all in vain'.

Katherine's parentage is almost as mysterious as the final part of her life was to be. Three years after her baptism another daughter of Richard Taylor was baptised, Jane, and her entry includes the information that her father was a doctor. His burial describes Richard Taylor as indeed a doctor and several times mayor of Thaxted. His son, also Richard, went to Caius College, Cambridge. Katherine must have been the child of his second marriage. His first wife was Barbara Purchas who died in 1591. In 1623 he was involved in an indenture with George Purchas, a relative of Thaxted's only literary celebrity, Samuel, in extending the provisions of the grammar school.

Samuel Purchas had been educated at Thaxted grammar school, gone on to Cambridge and become vicar of Eastwood. In 1613 he published the first part of his *Purchas his Pilgrimage or Relations of the World and the Religions Observed in all Ages*

and *Places Discovered from the Creation to the Present Time.*
Not until 1625 did he publish the final volume which included
the account of the shipwreck in the Bermudas that Shakespeare
seems to have read in manuscript and used as part of the plot of
The Tempest.

From Thaxted to the Bermudas is a long voyage not just in
terms of the acres of water crossed through long weeks but in the
imagination. A similar background produced both Samuel
Purchas and William Shakespeare though Purchas had the
benefit of a longer formal education than his contemporary. He
kept in close touch with his family in Thaxted and perhaps some
of the Jarvisses heard portions of the miraculous voyages read
aloud. Two of them witnessed a deed for Absalom Onion, a
relative of Samuel Purchas, which mentions him and his London
house. I like to think that something of Shakespeare brushed the
Jarvisses even as remotely as he brushed the fortunate isles,
the Bermoothes.

There's no record of what happened to the baby John
Ackworth, spurious son, but the registers record the baptisms
and burials of his half-siblings, Mary, Helen, Joanna, Thomas
and another Mary. 'Cheats never prosper' was a saw I was
brought up with and no doubt the tongues wagged again and
the rapid deaths of all their children were seen as sufficient
evidence that John and Katherine Jarvis had cheated and were
being punished for it. There's no record of their own deaths in
the register so perhaps they moved away with their misfortune
and life was kinder to them elsewhere.

John's parents, Thomas and Helen, also disappear. There
seems to be a period at the beginning of the seventeenth century
when the vicar who had held his job since 1573, Thomas Crosby,
became, through age or disinclination, lax with the entries of
marriages and burials. There are eight years without any
marriages for the family and eleven years without burials, though
both of them had been running at the rate of one or two every
few years. At some point during this time both Thomas, son of
Thomas, and the charming Helen must have died, leaving
Thomas, son of John, to become the new Thomas senior.

Thomas junior who had married Mary Neale in 1593 was the
son of James. William Neale had paid twenty shillings on his
lands in the 1598 tax and was therefore a fairly substantial

citizen. James, Thomas's brother, to whom his grandfather had left the little black nag, married Agnes Rolf in 1599. Robert Rolf was the town clerk.

The death of Elizabeth I in 1603 meant an election. William Westley, the then mayor of Thaxted, wrote to Lord Rich saying that he would be at Chelmsford on March 5 or 6 to give his voice for Sir Francis Barrington and he attached a schedule of other freeholders whose 'concurrance' he had obtained. The schedule is unfortunately lost so that it can't now be known which of the Jarvisses were on it, and it may be in any case that they voted for Sir Francis's opponent, since a century later their votes went massively for the representative of the Mildmay family and therefore against the Barrington candidate.

Because of its various charities Thaxted parish had no need to collect a poor rate. Though this was a great advantage to the inhabitants, for the would-be historian it means that a vital house-to-house record, which would have established exactly how many and which Jarvis households there were at this time, simply doesn't exist. Rates were only collected when there was some special need such as the one for church repairs and the new bells of 1618, which shows James Jarvis living in the hamlet of Richmonds Green and Monk Street and Thomas Jarvis junior at Stanbrook End. It seems as if the rate was only levied on the richer or more willing inhabitants, since 'junior' implies that there was a Thomas Jarvis senior who didn't contribute.

Two new names appear about this time: Andrew born in 1599 and Daniel in 1612, both sons of a Thomas. Andrew appears only briefly in a rent roll of 1629, with Daniel and Thomas the elder and Thomas the younger. Daniel is the son of Thomas the younger, but Andrew is much more difficult to pin down. There's no record of him marrying or having children. He is possibly the Andrew Jarvis who died at Suers End, Saffron Walden, two years into the Civil War. Perhaps he is the brother of Daniel for his name is perpetuated in the family although he himself disappears. If so, his brothers and sisters include, as well as Daniel, Dorcas, Martha, Abraham and Isaac, the strong Biblical influence on the names suggesting that Thomas junior was firmly Protestant and possibly Puritan.

Thomas had inherited forty acres which James had bought from Sir John Cutt and they made him, in the manner of the day, a prosperous freeholder. Since, as I've explained, there were no rates in Thaxted, the manor rolls often provide the only evidence, apart from wills, of who lived where. Unfortunately the picture is far from complete and especially so for the Jarvisses during the early years of Stuart rule, when the rolls were particularly fragmentary and those for the smaller manors of Priors Hall and Richmonds, which covered part of the area near the junction of the river Chelmer and the Stanbrook where the family mostly lived, are missing altogether.

The reign of James I is curiously formless and difficult to grasp. Historians have censured him for what he didn't do internationally, for his failure to support the Protestant cause in Europe. Yet at home, however people might have murmured about this, they prospered in peace. Certainly the Jarvisses did and they must be typical of a very high percentage of the population. In this period, when I know, and when history records, least of them, they were quietly building on that foundation of unostentatious enoughness that they had begun in the reigns of the Tudors. They were marrying and having children, acquiring small parcels of land, making a living that brought a certain degree of comfort with some interest in what they were doing, voting, leaving wills, taking a part in their community. These aren't spectacular achievements. They are the tapestry of everyday life when it doesn't include Mars, god of war, and they are what modern individualistic capitalism, tempered by a little social welfare, aspires to: everyone doing his own thing, cultivating his own cottage garden. The English late twentieth-century character was certainly prefigured in this reign if not exactly laid down, for the yeomen and husbandmen formed a rural middle class whose values have hardly changed, although translated into suburbia and modern technology, and these are the majority values of our present society. They may be summed up as the attainment of the highest possible degree of comfort and security and a concern for one's immediate domestic circle. They are the commonsense virtues based on common animal traits and it can't really be alleged that there is anything specifically human about them. Nor is there anything particularly yeomanlike, since the aspiration to achieve them was shared equally by the labourers whom the yeomen employed.

However, two movements were swelling which were to affect

this, on the surface, placid, secure life and both of them were man-made. Animals don't as far as we know invent religious structures of organised churches and dogmas. The religio-social aspirations of the artisans and labourers and the religio-political aspirations of the gentry and aristocracy were shortly to nip the rural middle class between them. In a world turned upside down like an egg-timer, it was hard to retain a safe place in the middle as the backbone of the nation.

Thomas Jarvis (but which one?) paid his taxes dutifully in 1626 for the new King Charles of twenty shillings and four pence, when it seemed that the long peace at home was over and that the French might invade at Harwich. Landguard fort had fallen into decay since Elizabeth died and money was needed to repair it, for the coast was very vulnerable to attack. Several of the gentry refused to pay the subsidy, as many people of all ranks had refused to respond to James's attempt to raise a loan in 1604. Meanwhile the contingent of Essex troops for the Cadiz expedition had mutinied against their conductor while waiting to embark at Plymouth. Essex had already lost many men in the proposed expedition to recover the Palatinate for Protestantism and James's son-in-law, the Elector Frederick, when hundreds had died miserably without food or shelter at the siege of Breda in 1624. The days of Elizabeth suddenly seemed golden again with the last turbulent years of her reign forgotten like the miseries of childhood.

A silent, or largely so, revolt was already beginning all over Essex, as men refused to turn out for the musters of the trained bands or to pay the subsidy, towns refused to supply men or armour or protested about the soldiers billeted on them, usually on 'poor persons who are already half undone,' since 'persons of better ability absolutely refuse to receive them'. The year before, the Privy Council had recommended that the Irish soldiers, who, it was alleged, had assaulted the women and plundered the men of Maldon, should be moved elsewhere: 'we hold Thacsted the fittest, if there be no soldiers there billetted already.'

There was restlessness too directed against the Dutch cloth-workers in the county. A company of clothworkers had been incorporated in Colchester in 1618 to deal with the problem, but five years later the local weavers were still petitioning for help. There was also renewed hostility to Catholics, particularly at the threat of invasion, and 'great assemblies of popish recusants' were reported about Harwich in 1625.

Thaxted had its own Catholic recusant family: the Wisemans, who owned the manors of Yardleys, Broadoaks, and part of Horham too for a period, and these were confiscated for a long time, beginning in the last years of Elizabeth, when John Donne's mother suffered in the same way, though this didn't stop Lady Wiseman intervening, when the town sought a renewal of its charter in 1617, to point out that certain of the privileges which the town was claiming belonged of right to her son as lord of the manor of Yardleys.

In 1623 John Jarvis was called twice to the Quarter Sessions at Chelmsford to do jury service. Presumably this was the John who had married Katherine Ackworth, for John senior had died in 1616, the last survivor of old Thomas's sons. As well as the usual assortment of Thomases there were also at least three Jameses, a Joseph and an Andrew all heading Jarvis households in Thaxted. One James was the son of John senior, one the son of Thomas senior and one the son of bewitched James whose son, also James, was married and fathering children. In these circumstances it's impossible to draw the neat family tree beloved of the old style genealogists; the family has to be treated as a whole, as a kind of nursery of seedlings or a coppice of saplings sprung from fruits fallen from the same parent and in their turn letting drop their seeds.

In 1632 Elleanor, wife of Thomas senior, died, followed a few months later by her husband. In his will he mentions four children: James, who is the eldest and is to have the lion's share, Thomas, a daughter Agnes and a son Richard. Thomas the elder, as his will calls him, is designated 'husbandman', which suggests that his 'tenement wherein I dwell with the appurtenances with all yards, gardens and outyards . . . situate . . . in the parish of Thaxted near a common field called Stonywork' is only leased, not freehold. He also bequeaths a little piece of land in Stonywork 'containing one rood more or less'. It has been suggested by one local historian that Stonywork was a corruption of Stanbrook but since the two names existed side by side this seems unlikely and if it is so the name must be a piece of Thaxted humour. No doubt Stonywork was just what its name implies and part of a long verbal line that included in my childhood stony broke.

Thomas also left three pounds of 'lawful English money' to be paid to Thomas Crow within three years after his death. In 1612 Thomas Crow had married Elleanor Jarvis, who had been born in 1589, perhaps the first child of Elleanor and Thomas. Thomas Crow, son of Thomas and Elleanor, had been baptised in 1616 and would therefore now be a young man of twenty-six. Perhaps this three pounds was the remainder from his mother's marriage settlement. The Crows were an old Thaxted family who were already settled there in the fourteenth century.

Agnes was to have 6s 8d, a noble, every year for six years. Richard was to have twenty shillings within four years of his father's death. Neither of these two appears again. James and Thomas, however, did homage for their lands at the manor court and paid their fine on inheritance. Then they sold, or 'alienated' as the term was, the little piece of land of one rood to Christopher Waltham alias Tanner.

It's surprising to us now how many people in a little town like Thaxted were alias something. We tend to think of an alias as the badge of a criminal but in Thaxted there were at least a dozen families who had two names by which they regularly appeared until the eighteenth century, when the custom began to die out and most settled for one or the other.

Thomas senior left all his 'goods and chattels, household stuffs and implements' to be divided equally among his children. Unlike earlier members of the family he left nothing to be given to the poor. That custom as far as the Jarvisses were concerned had utterly died out. Thomas is the first to mention in the introduction to his will that Thaxted is in the diocese of London. The preamble to the worldly bequests is also more elaborate: 'first and principally I commend my soul into the hands of almighty God assuredly trusting to be saved by the precious death and passion of Jesus Christ my only saviour and redeemer and my body to the earth from whence it came to be buried in Christian burial.'

The Laudian influence rather than the Puritan is at work here. The vicar of Little Bardfield in Elizabeth's time had merely committed his 'soul to almighty God and my body to be buried in Christian burial'. Old Thomas Jarvis gave his soul 'into the hands of God Almighty my only Creator and Redeemer' and his

60

body to Christian burial. I think it would be a mistake to infer from the later Thomas's will, however, that he was necessarily what would now be called High Church, although it's clear he wasn't a dissenter or he would have objected to such a formula. Rather I think it's an indication of the shift in the Church itself which had so permeated the legal and political establishment that even the wills of ordinary people who were members of the Established Church took on a new phraseology and flavour. The preamble probably reflects more the official views of Robert Spilmay, one of the witnesses, whose hand seems to have drawn the will than those precisely of Thomas Jarvis. The emphasis on the body returning to the earth from 'whence it came' has a ring of John Donne about it although his own will contains no such phrase but as might be expected makes a prose poem by redrafting the accepted phrases. Curiously enough it is the will of Donne's father, made in 1575, half a century before, that comes closest to Thomas Jarvis's of 1632, though even that doesn't have the dust to dust, ashes to ashes image so firmly embedded in it.

The year after Thomas senior died, a Thomas Jarvis was elected one of the constables by the manor court. It seems likely that this was the previous Thomas junior, become senior by the death of his cousin, since the job, although not popular, was usually filled by a yeoman, presumably because he had sufficient wealth and status to be able to do the job effectively and without being so liable to the corruption of bribery.

There's a lot to be said for an elected constabulary with responsible members of society each having to take their turn in dealing with local crime. It was easy enough for the gentry, who in theory were eligible to be chosen as constables but in practice managed to avoid it, to sneer at the village Dogberry when they saw him caricatured on stage, but in fact his was one of the most important posts in the community. He took an oath to arrest rioters, breakers of the King's peace, felons and counterfeiters, rogues, vagabonds and nightwalkers, to raise the hue and cry, to oversee inns and alehouses, arrest popish recusants, maintain archery and issue the summons for the muster of the trained bands. Thus his duties extended through the criminal, religious and defence spheres, to social welfare, in helping those with a licence to beg, or to community aid, in getting in the harvest or mending bridges. Along with the churchwardens he covered most of the duties now undertaken by local and national welfare services. Again, there's much to be said for a police force which isn't absorbingly concerned with crime. This first recorded Thomas Jarvis constable served his term without mishap. A later one wasn't to be so efficient or, perhaps, so lucky.

A Thomas junior also died in 1632 and his widow Rebecca was granted the administration of his goods, which included a lease of manor lands. There's no record of their marriage but their son Thomas was baptised in 1629. Rebecca married again a few months after her first husband's death. Her new husband was Thomas Porter, son of the William who was several times mayor of Thaxted. In his will William described himself as 'gent' though he seems to have owned, but not worked, the windmill 'called the old mill' in Mill End, which he left to his sons Henry and Robert. To his son Samuel he left £150. Another property in a nearby village was to be sold by his executors and the money divided between William, Thomas, Robert, Laurence, Samuel and Elizabeth, his children 'parte and parte like' after the mortgage was paid off. His bed and bedding 'lying standing in the chamber over the kitchen nigh the window there' were to go to Henry, as well as two suits, one of which 'is my worst' and the other 'which Thomas Darkley hath now to make'. Thomas was to have the rest of his 'wearing apparel together with my gown'. Laurence had the residue of his goods, chattels, hay, corn and cattle.

By the time of his father's will in 1642 Thomas had moved with Rebecca to Great Dunmow where their children were baptised. In his will Thomas described himself as yeoman and, where his father had made an elaborate religious preamble calling on the Trinity and invoking the 'death and passion of Jesus Christ' to blot out his sins and bequeathing his body 'to the earth from whence it was first framed hoping and verily believing that at the last and general day of judgement it shall come to judgement and rise again with all flesh', Thomas embarks at once and starkly 'concerning my temporal estate'.

He seems to have owned three properties: the one he lived in, which he presumably left to his wife Rebecca, and two which he left one each to his sons Thomas and Samuel. He also divided his silver buttons equally between his sons. Thomas was left his cloak and Samuel his best breeches. The rest of his clothes went to his brother Henry, while daughter Rebecca was given his best bed with all its furnishings 'standing in the chamber called the prison chamber' and six of his best cushions.

There is a formula which, with variations, is used in wills of the time to introduce a warning proviso: 'And my will and mind is that . . .' Thomas wished to ensure that two sums of ten pounds each left to his grandchildren, William and Thomas, should reach them safely. He therefore threatens his son Thomas, their father, with the loss of the piece of property bequeathed to him unless the money is paid to the boys when they reach twenty-two years of age. He also leaves them a gold ring apiece for their immediate use, presumably as a memento.

Thomas Porter senior died in January 1670 and was taken back to Thaxted to be buried. Rebecca lived until 1679 and was then buried in Great Dunmow. In the hearth tax for 1671 she is rated for seven hearths or chimneys, which suggests a very substantial house. The Thaxted property which had belonged to her Jarvis husband passed to Thomas Porter, then back to her on his death and thence to Thomas Jarvis who could be her son by her first husband or another of the family. I incline to believe that Thomas, his father, was a son, the eldest, of Thomas junior who, bizarrely, only became 'senior' in the year that his own son died. The lands that the widow Porter paid rent for lay among those of Thomas, now senior's, known children, Isaac, Abraham, Martha and Daniel.

Their mother Mary died in 1633. That same year the churchwardens, no doubt in conjunction with constable Jarvis, laid in a store of powder and shot. There had been another serious famine at the beginning of the decade, with rioting in Colchester, where the poor people were said to be 'ready to famish'. The religio-political situation was worsening as Laud tried to impose his version of conformity on the Established Church, and Puritan Essex dug in its heels against what it saw as popery and idolatry: the surplice, communion rails and bowing and scraping in church.

Thaxted was obliged to renew its charter in 1637 in one of the King's desperate efforts to raise money; James Jarvis paid two shillings towards the required sum and one of the Thomases, presumably senior, paid six shillings and eightpence. However, when the notorious Ship Money was levied the same year only

Joseph, who held property in the next door parishes of Lindsell and Great Easton, contributed anything, though it has been estimated that about 20,000 people were assessed in Essex, some for as little as tuppence halfpenny, so that several of the Thaxted family should have been eligible but deliberately defaulted along with their neighbours. Thaxted still hadn't paid up in 1639. The mayor was called to account by the Council of State but the town had found what looks like a piece of communal tax-dodging by entering into a legal wrangle with the next door parish of Wimbish about which of them was to include the manor of Yardleys in its returns. A note of exasperation can be heard in the letters to the Sheriff among the State Papers.

That same year Abraham, who seems to have been the eldest of Thomas senior's sons, married a local girl, Mary Overall. Joseph had married a girl called Joan some time before 1622 when they had a daughter, followed by a son Thomas six years later and another daughter Priscilla who was born and died in 1636. Joseph had prospered although it's not at all clear how or why. When he died in 1649 he made a will which must be quite deliberate in its invocation of 'the everliving, holy, blessed and glorious Trinity, father, son and holy ghost' at a time when Puritanism and indeed Unitarianism were in the ascendancy. His contribution to Ship Money gains added emphasis from this will.

He had purchased two properties which he left to his wife Joan for the rest of her life. One, at Sibleys Green, was then to go to his son Thomas; the other, a piece of arable land in Great Aversie Common, was to go to daughter Mary, together with twenty pounds and a third of all his household stuff, to be delivered to her one month after his wife's death or on the day of Mary's marriage whichever was the sooner. 'Provided always and nevertheless upon this condition following and my will and plain meaning is . . .' Here came the sting in the bequest. If she should at any time 'take to husband Thomas Saggers the younger, husbandman, or in any other manner or kind have to do with the said Thomas', the bequest should 'cease, determine and be utterly frustrate, void and of no effect' and the land, money and goods would all go to Thomas.

Was this just a simple case of a yeoman father feeling that a husbandman wasn't good enough for his daughter or was there a religious or political difference as well? Mary was obviously in love with young Thomas and her father had refused his consent. She was twenty-seven and her chance was slipping away. What was she to do?

Reader, she married him. She and Thomas eloped to High Roding two years after her father's death, where theirs was the only marriage recorded that year, presumably a precaution against the allegation that they weren't married at all. From Thomas Saggers' own will it's clear that she had forfeited the land and probably the other things as well. There's nothing in the religious preamble to the will to suggest a difference of faith from his father-in-law. What is clear, though, is that among their children Thomas and Mary had one boy for whom special provision had to be made because he was either mentally or physically handicapped. The house is left to Mary and their daughter Martha during their lives as long as they look after him, then to son Thomas and last to Robert, both with the same proviso. The boy outlived his mother, and by a few months his sister Martha, who died in February 1720. He died in the following August, perhaps missing her care. They had called him Joseph after his grandfather.

IV   *The Great Fight*

I've had to jump ahead in order to tie up the story that began with Joseph Jarvis's will made during the Civil War or, perhaps I should say, even earlier when Mary Jarvis fell in love with Thomas Saggers over seventy years before; and in doing so I have had inescapably to illustrate the cliché of time as an indivisible river which we dam or cut into understandable sections only with the artificial structure of what we call history.

It's almost impossible to say what the Jarvisses did in the great civil war which engulfed the country in 1642 but the chances are that some of them both served in the early stages and paid towards the upkeep of the Parliamentary forces. Unfortunately the very detailed returns which show Joseph and Daniel Jarvis paying up on their Lindsell property in 1641 are completely missing for Thaxted (perhaps once again the town had refused to pay) and the accounts of the later Commonwealth collectors show only the overall sums, £115 . 14s in 1644 for Thaxted, but without any personal assessments.

In the early years of the war men were levied from the trained bands to fight against the Royalists as far away as Berkshire, and this led eventually to a near mutiny of Essex men. 'Yesterday they were like to have killed their major general and they have hurt him in the face; such men are only fit for a gallows here and a hell hereafter,' Sir William Waller wrote of them in July 1643 and the major general, Richard Browne, feared that they would no longer march anywhere 'except homeward'.

Fortunately some of those in command were more under-standing than Waller and realized that, not being trained soldiers but farmers, the levies were better sent home where they could be more use raising crops and money, and they were disbanded. Even in the middle of a civil war it was recognised that by tradition the trained bands were to protect their own country and that military service mustn't be allowed to interfere with important seasonal tasks like getting in the harvest.

Essex had been quick to declare itself for Parliament, led by a majority among its gentry, and to form the Eastern Association with Cambridge, Hertfordshire, Suffolk and Norfolk. Several of its ministers had already clashed with Archbishop Laud on matters of religion, and soldiers billeted in the county before the war began had torn down communion rails and put the altar table back in the middle of the chancel at Stebbing before marching on to Dunmow.

Thaxted itself had its own religious excitements. The old vicar Newman Leader was put out by the Parliament and the living sequestrated. He had been vicar since 1612, brought up his children in Thaxted, taken an interest in the grammar school, going to Cambridge to buy books for it, and kept clear records including a dispensation to George Purchas to eat meat in Lent because he was ill. But Leader was an independent man who had fought both the Maynards, as lords of the manor, and the burgesses of the town over the matter of tithes.

It may seem unspiritual for a minister to concern himself so much with money and it might be tempting to see this as a particularly offensive aspect of the High Church clergy under Laud, but the truth is that the diary of Ralph Joslin, puritan vicar of Earls Colne throughout the Commonwealth period, shows exactly the same obsession. It wasn't necessarily the clergy of either colour, but the system whereby they had to wring their salaries out of the local people by tithes, that was wrong, and the Commonwealth Government partly recognised this in its scheme of augmenting the local income from other sources.

When he was expelled in 1643 there was, it seems, little help for Leader from Thaxted people and the experience perhaps hastened his death two years later. Some of the townspeople had already ridden the twelve miles to Earls Colne and asked Ralph Joslin to accept the sequestration as soon as Leader was put out but although he went and preached there he refused the living. The Committee of Plundered Ministers put in Thomas Mall who published in 1645, presumably while still at Thaxted, *A Cloud of Witnesses; or, The Sufferer's Mirror; made up of the swan-like songs and other choice passages of several Martyrs and Confessors* to the Sixteenth Century, in their *Treatises, Letters, Prayers, in their Prisons and Exiles, at the Bar or Stake*, which in its very title gives so much the flavour of the times.

However, on the death of Newman Leader, the dowager Lady Maynard exercised her late husband's right to make an appointment to the living and instituted one Edmund Croxton, 'a man for swearing, cursing and drunkenness, the whole country cannot parallel'. Clearly Lady Maynard was playing a royalist game of her own and led by Thomas Mall, those parishioners who were for the Parliament took immediate action 'perceiving what a judgement they lay under to sit under such a soul starving pastor'.

Croxton was called before the Committee for Plundered Ministers in May 1646 and the living taken from him. Lady Maynard was given permission to make a new appointment since she alleged that Croxton had resigned the living to her before it was taken away, a fiction clearly cooked up between them. Meanwhile the 'well affected' parishioners, as they were called, had sent a new delegation to Ralph Joslin asking him to come to their parish but he, making the usual modest excuse about his 'unfitness', advised them 'to consider how to make the place comfortable for a minister,' thus indirectly justifying Newman Leader's long struggles over the tithes.

Lady Maynard now presented Samuel Hall, who had been in prison for preaching against the Parliament at Cambridge, and the parishioners petitioned the committee against his appointment, alleging among other things that Lady Maynard had already cost them a hundred pounds in prosecuting her unworthy ministers. Three times Hall was summoned before the Assembly of Divines and found unfit. He then appealed to the House of Lords, who, when they asked the Assembly for its opinion of him, were told that 'this very man hath occasioned more trouble to us, and more hindered the public service than any other minister that ever was referred to us'. The Lords were at first satisfied with this but then, presumably under pressure from the Maynards, they again asked the Assembly of Divines to show cause why Hall shouldn't be instituted and this time the case was put, on June 4, by a delegation from the Assembly led by the vicar of Finchingfield, Stephen Marshall, one of the most prominent Puritans, a co-author of the Smectymnuus pamphlet and acquaintance of Milton (his bones were to be dug up from their grave in Westminster Abbey after the Restoration and thrown into a pit with those of, among others, Cromwell's mother and daughter).

This might have been the end of Hall's attempt to get into the living but the insurrection of the London apprentices and the army's resolution to march on London to restore order gave the Maynards an opportunity for a last try. Lady Maynard must have been ill, for she died on August 5, but on the 3rd her son Lord William took advantage of the national confusion to pass an order through a depleted House of Lords, which was sitting illegally without its speaker, for the institution of Hall. The order was carried to Thaxted but the first act of the reconstituted Parliament was to pass an ordinance annulling all orders and votes taken in both Houses while their speakers were absent from July 26 to August 6 and then to impeach those members, including Lord Maynard, who had tried to sit without them.

As soon as the parliamentary side received a copy of this ordinance they took it to the church where they met Samuel Hall, the mayor, Michael Nightingale and the town clerk, Henry Jebb, on their way to service. However, when shown the ordinance these three refused to accept it and Hall and Jebb, 'in fighting manner said it did nothing concern Mr Hall', and Hall went into the church and preached both morning and afternoon. Jebb unwisely added that those who had presented the ordinance, the sequestrators as they are called, were always troubling them with such frivolous things.

On August 15 another attempt was made to present the ordinance. Hall had come to the church with the mayor and several others of the 'disaffected' royalist party in the morning to preach. The sequestrators had demanded his authority. Hall had said that they shouldn't question it and had proceeded to preach. In the afternoon the sequestrators had blocked his way up into the pulpit and again demanded his authority, which he refused to produce. Then Christopher Tanner, a churchwarden, and Edward Mountford threatened to pull the sequestrators out of the pulpit and 'said that Mr Hall should preach too with other daring words'.

Next the mayor intervened, not to restore order but to reprove the sequestrators for making such a disturbance which so 'animated' divers disaffected men and women 'that they fell upon the sequestrators, beat them, tore the hair from their heads, their bands from their necks, endangering the taking away their lives. Ann, the wife of Thomas Meade; Elizabeth the daughter of the said Thomas Meade, the wife of Lawrence Porter, the wife of Nathaniel Westley, the wife of Samuel Salmon; these women fell violently upon the said sequestrators . . . tore their hats and cloaks off, then came Henry Jebb, Thos Meade junr, Edward Meade junr, John Moore (who struck Captain Turner one of the sequestrators), William Caton, Lewis Caton, Nathaniel Smith alias Baily, John Grey and John Baker who animated and abetted the said women'. When a move was made to intervene, mayor Nightingale said, 'Let them alone and let the women decide the case.' The sequestrators were 'forced to haste as fast as they could out of the church being in danger of their lives', for the women 'straddled over the pews' and broke the iron stand that held the big hourglass for timing the sermon and would have struck them with it.

Captain Turner was not necessarily a coward though it isn't clear if he or another Captain Turner had led the local troops in the early stages of the Civil War when the King was winning, and was to fight again at Colchester. But that was against soldiers not against a band of harridans, as they would have been called in my childhood when the tradition by which the women did the fighting, on the grounds that the courts would treat them more leniently, had dwindled to the occasional but recognized and almost ritualized female violence which always involved tearing the opponent's hair and usually clawing and scratching. Such women were frowned on by their neighbours as 'not respectable', coarse and unwomanly.

The sequestrators complained to the House of Lords and presented their affidavits on August 27. Immediately the Lords made an order that those complained of should be attached and brought to the bar of the house, and a messenger was sent to arrest them. Michael Nightingale was over seventy, so infirm that he couldn't ride and therefore had to walk over thirty miles. On September 8 an order was made for the case to be heard the following Thursday and the mayor, town clerk and others were bailed. This was of little use to them, however, since they couldn't have got home to Thaxted and back in time for the new trial, and they petitioned for the case to be heard. In keeping with the law's delays, the trial was again put off for a week and it wasn't until the 24th that the Lords pronounced that Samuel Hall's order was indeed void and that he should not preach at Thaxted any more and that Henry Jebb 'for his contemptuous words against the Parliament' should be committed to the Fleet prison 'during the pleasure of this House'.

There must have been consternation among the delinquents and certainly all the fight had gone out of them, for they hurried to prepare their humble submissions which they presented three days later. 'Some of the men have been a month in durance, others, husbandmen in time of seed, and women from their children, are here at great charge. Another of the petitioners has no subsistence but his daily labour and his family are in great distress in his absence; they are heartily sorry for their offences and pray for their discharge.'

Their Lordships were merciful: all the rest, apart from the mayor and Hall, were discharged, having submitted. Nightingale was bidden to attend them the following day, when he was presumably given a good talking to and sent home. Hall himself, who had been in custody under Black Rod, made his petition on October 1 and was released too. He was heartily sorry, promised not to interfere in Thaxted again and prayed to be discharged to seek some way to maintain himself, being 'in great want'. Attached to his petition are documents affirming his imprisonment two years before for preaching at Trinity College, Cambridge against the government and a certificate of blasphemous words used by him in another sermon. Milton would have called him a 'blind mouth . . . such as for their bellies' sake / Creep and intrude and climb into the fold'.

> And when they list, their lean and flashy songs
> Grate on their scannel pipes of wretched straw,
> The hungry sheep look up, and are not fed,
> But swoln with wind, and the rank mist they draw,
> Rot inwardly, and foul contagion spread . . .

The Assembly of Divines had mentioned in their report on Hall how such as he were trying to get back into a living.

The town was obviously as deeply divided as the rest of the country, and split into two factions whose members were often closely linked not just by religion and politics but by blood. Michael Nightingale, whose family were glovers, had been churchwarden with Nathaniel Westley to the deposed vicar Newman Leader. Nat Westley had married Elizabeth Leader. Laurence Porter was of course the brother of Thomas Porter who married Rebecca Jarvis and the son of a former mayor. Laurence had married Elizabeth Collyn in 1610 and when the great fight took place she was nearly sixty.

Captain Richard Turner in contrast was only twenty-two. He belonged to a well-established Thaxted family described as 'gent' in their wills and 'Mr' in the registers. They ran to classical names: Augustine, Alexander, Cesar. Richard's father was Augustine. One of his witnesses was his unmarried aunt Rose, daughter of Alexander. Turner's fellow sequestrators included John Heywood, whose wife left some money in her will to a son of the third, Andrew Halls, whose family were tanners.

The Halls, Turners and Christopher Tanner, the obstreperous churchwarden, had all adjacent property at Stanbrook, next to Thomas Jarvis, and there was perhaps an element of neighbourly dissent added to the political difference. Will Caton, one of Nightingale's party, was a blacksmith, a violent man who had threatened the constables with a hammer when they tried to press him for Captain Turner's troop in 1643. Almost twenty years before a Turner had married a Caton girl so there may also have been a family feud element in his intervention.

Of the other witnesses against Nightingale, one, John Brown, was also left a small legacy in Susan Heywood's will, while the other, John Humphrey, was a substantial property owner who had been a churchwarden with Nightingale in 1637. All this makes it hard to see where the lines of dispute lay. Nightingale's party was that of the Lord of the Manor and several of its members had been pillars of the old establishment. Turner's party were mainly from the Thaxted middle classes and it's possible that they resented not only the choice of ministers but the patron's right to choose. Samuel Hall managed to creep back into favour and became first curate and eventually vicar at Great Bardfield.

When Ralph Joslin had been asked to bring such another divided town together over their choice of minister he wrote: 'Oh woeful sad divisions . . . both parts stiff, divided, a most sad town . . .' Thaxted was without a vicar for a few months. During this time the plans were drawn up for replacing the old episcopal system with the presbyterian, and a convenient list of parishes with vicars and elders remains; for Thaxted, Edward Mead and Simon Horndon were the elders. In 1648 the *Essex Testimony* was drawn up and the new appointee, James Parkin, signed his name to it as vicar of Thaxted, in support of conformity and the Solemn League and Covenant. In 1650 he was described as 'a quiet man and taketh great pains in his calling'. His stipend was augmented by the Committee for Plundered Ministers, incidentally bearing out both Newman Leader's and Ralph Joslin's contention that the cure was underpaid at an estimated £70 a year, and when Parliament instituted the system of civil registrars in 1653 he was chosen to fill the post.

From the time of his installation as vicar the Parkins have a long history in Thaxted for, although James himself was driven out after the Restoration, what must be his son James was married by 1675 when his first child was baptised, and the baptisms and burials continue down into the nineteenth century, as far as the Sara Parkin, née Gilder, whose great brown teapot was bequeathed to Minnie Jarvis and eventually stood proudly on Maud's piano.

James Parkin seems to have at least temporarily healed some of the divisions shown up by the great fight in the Church, for a reconciled Christopher Tanner was one of the Parliament's tax collectors of money for the Irish war, along with among others Alexander Turner.

Not surprisingly the church registers reflect all the unrest. The burials and christenings hold up quite well in numbers, since the dead had to be buried whatever else went on, and people seemed to feel, at least in the early forties, that children had to be baptised. Yet even these essential services collapsed in 1647 during the tumult over Samuel Hall, until James Parkin signed the register as vicar in December.

The most spectacular fall was in marriages which dropped from their usual figure of about fifteen a year before the war to four in 1644 and only one in 1646 and 1650. Five years later there were twenty-five. Obviously, with the ascendancy of Presbyterianism and the end of toleration for non-conformity, many people hurried to catch up and regularize their existing relationships. But it's interesting that they had felt no compelling need to do so without the strong arm of the law as applied by the major generals.

Some of the earlier marriages may have been private ones and it would be interesting to know what form they took. Ralph Joslin mentions a wedding at which he preached and 'married them in a method that gave great content to honest people'. One of the functions of the wedding ceremony was for the family and friends of the groom to give the couple a flying start with lavish gifts. On this occasion the groom took £56, a tidy sum, over half the vicar's annual stipend.

The registers chart an interesting piece of Puritan sexual licence for the Jarvis family. In 1644, presumably during the brief cure of Thomas Mall, Joan Bocock took her bastard child to be baptised Thomas. Incredulously the entry records that according to her testimony its father was Thomas Jarvis, 'septuagenarian'. This must be the son of bewitched James who was now seventy-two. There are no other Bocock appearances in the registers, so it looks as if Joan was a servant girl from outside Thaxted living in with the family. Joslin paid his girl Susan Hadley 40s a year and four pairs of shoes.

Thomas's wife Mary had been dead for eleven years. The tone of the entry suggests either that the vicar was amazed by the virility of the seventy-year-old or that he thought the girl was lying in the hope of getting some money from the old man. Presumably she took her child back to wherever she had come from, since neither of them appears in Thaxted again.

Meanwhile Thomas's other children were marrying and having children of their own. Isaac married Susan Purchas in 1646 in Little Easton, Martha had married Henry Badcock before 1635, Daniel married Joan Morell in 1642 and Abraham, who was a miller, was married too. Just in case the picture was becoming too simple with this variety of names, Thomas Jarvis junior, whose wife Elizabeth had died leaving him with two daughters, married again in 1640, a girl who had also been married before, Mary Winterflood. In addition James and Frances, who had married some time before 1627, had the last of their six recorded daughters in 1641.

A manor roll of 1646 shows four Jarvis freeholders: Isaac, Daniel, Thomas the elder and James the elder, and a Thomas

Jarvis paying the four days' carriage work rent of £1 . 6s . 8d. That year the damask roses were out early. Ralph Joslin had buds in his garden by mid-April and a 'full ripe and blown damask' on May 20. But the early spring was followed by an equally early winter: September was 'a marvellous wet season, winter coming on very early and the wet continued until December'. The wheat which was 'exceedingly smitten, dwindled and lank' rotted in the fields and the pastures were trampled into mud by the cattle. Meat, butter and cheese were dear, wool soared to over sixteen pence a pound and work was 'very dead', both because of that and because no winter wheat or rye could be sown. The scarcity and high prices led to 'great divisions and fears of our utter ruin in the Kingdom'. Only the hops did well.

It was the beginning of a run of six bad harvests which more perhaps than anything else were to destroy the Commonwealth and make men long to bring back the monarchy, for surely scarcity was God's punishment on men's sins, as was all other adversity, and their chief sin was rebellion. While the Lords were debating the affairs of Thaxted, Joslin noted a time of great sickness, agues and spotted fever, cattle dying of murrain and fruit rotting on the trees. Food was dearer than ever: beef went up a penny a pound to threepence, butter was sixpence ha'penny, cheese fourpence, currants ninepence, sugar eighteenpence and the essential candle sevenpence. The two staples for bread and beer, wheat and malt, were eight shillings and four shillings a bushel. The poor as usual suffered most while yeomen like the Jarvisses though no doubt they complained of the high prices were able to profit by them when they were the sellers not the buyers. Indeed, apart from luxuries like currants and sugar, they must have been largely self-sufficient. Those two items make me wonder whether one of the highlights of my childhood, the current pudding boiled in a cloth and eaten hot or cold in slices with butter and sugar, was invented at this time or has an even older lineage.

Abraham Jarvis had bought or built himself a watermill at Stanbrook. Traditionally millers thrived when wheat was scarce and prices were high and he seems to have been no exception. His first two children had been baptised while Newman Leader was vicar but after that he seems to have given up infant baptism and when one of them was buried in 1649 it was nameless, as many of the children buried at this time were. Because child mortality was so high people often developed an ambiguous attitude to cope with it. The desperate ignorance of even the university-educated made such an attitude even more necessary. Joslin writing two years before the death of Abraham's nameless child says: 'The night again my son very ill; he did not cry so much as the night before; whether the cause was want of strength I know not; he had a little froth in his mouth continually; in the morning there came some red mattery stuff out of his mouth which made us apprehend his throat might be sore . . . This day my dear babe Ralph quietly fell asleep and is at rest with the Lord. This correction though sad was seasoned with present goodness, for first the Lord had given it us until both my wife and I had gotten strength, and so more fit to bear it than in the depth of our sickness; the Lord gave us time to bury it in our thoughts; we looked on it as a dying child three or four days; three it died quietly without shrieks or sobs or sad groans; it breathed out the soul with nine gasps; it was the youngest and our affections not so wonted unto it.' It was ten days old.

The war came in earnest to Essex in June 1648 when a party of royalists under Sir Charles Lucas and Sir George Lisle barricaded themselves into the town of Colchester and Sir Thomas Fairfax sat down around it in a siege that lasted several weeks. Captain Turner went at once to the siege and so did another officer from Thaxted, Thomas Morrell. Both sent back warrants to the constables for the troops under their command to march to the leaguer, as the siege was called. Both warrants were discovered a few years ago in the chimney of a house in Thaxted.

The chimney was a favourite hiding place for centuries until blocked up to accommodate modern heating. These two concealed papers may have been hidden at the Restoration or immediately after they were received by the constables. If the latter they testify again to the divided loyalties of the town but also show an unbelievable naivety. Perhaps the recipients hoped the siege would be over before the troops could be sent for again. If so they must have been disappointed. And how did they explain the failure of the troops to arrive and the missing warrants?

If on the other hand they were hidden at the Restoration, rather than simply destroyed, it must have been out of the perennial desire to avoid responsibility by claiming that one was only following orders. Lucas and Lisle, both of whom were shot after the town surrendered, became royalist heroes and it was probably as well to have had no hand in the provision of troops that led to their defeat, after weeks when the inhabitants were forced to eat horseflesh and even rats as Fairfax tightened the siege. 'The carts went continually to the leaguer and so did persons, that there was no distinction made of the Sabbath, so that war truly is ready to make people more vile, a rare thing to see men made better.'

If the Thaxted draft-dodgers escaped with the connivance of, at least, one of the constables they were lucky, for the parliamentary losses were heavy and the whole siege was fought in that curse of soldiers through the ages continual rain, 'the season sad and threatening', with floods, 'the hay rotted in the fields, the corn pulled down with weeds' and the whole country undone by the 'sad change of the war'. Joslin noted 'the divisions among ourselves, our cryings-out after peace on any terms to save our skins and estate, whatsoever become of others'. He had himself been plundered of almost everything movable and forced to flee with only the clothes he and his family stood up in by the royalist band on its way to Colchester.

The surrender coupled with Cromwell's defeat of the Scots saved the revolution for the time being. Now someone must save the peace, as Milton saw, writing on Colchester and Fairfax's success '. . . what can war but endless war still breed . . . ?'

In vain doth valour bleed
While avarice and rapine share the land . . .

However amid all these turmoils the Horham manor courts were still held and in 1649 Thomas and James duly entered into possession of the lands that had belonged to their father James who had died in 1648. Three years later a lengthy rental was drawn up showing some of old Thomas's lands lying between those of Christopher Tanner and Richard Turner like a buffer state.

Old Thomas was still paying the same rent, twenty-three and fourpence, for his forty acres that his father James had paid over seventy-five years before. The lands were still scattered in parcels and indeed the rest of the family's holdings show that integration into large groupings had made only slight progress. Men were still buying strips in the common fields for plough or pasture. Abraham and Isaac shared such a piece between them, next to a bit owned by their father in Cursall Common field, and Daniel and Isaac shared another which their father seems to have given previously to Andrew, who had either died, although there's no record of his burial, or moved away. Old Thomas also owned land near the big farm called Broadfann's which belonged indeed to the Fann family and was described as a 'capital messuage'. It had once been taken over during Elizabeth's reign by a raiding party of neighbours, a not uncommon happening.

Martha, old Thomas's daughter, and her husband and son, both called Henry Badcock, had a house and four acres that had once belonged to John Jarvis next to the two acres belonging to Thomas Jarvis the younger. Typically the four acres were split into two parcels and so were the two acres. The picture is still very much of earlier strip cultivation or of the present-day small-farmer agriculture of the continent.

Once again there was a Thomas the elder and a Thomas the younger. But not for long. The following year old Thomas gave up his pursuit of servant maids (perhaps like King David he found their young flesh could no longer warm him) and his lands were divided amongst his children, including Rebecca Porter, presumably to have for her lifetime and then to pass to her son, Thomas Jarvis, or his son. The old man left no will, so his wishes have to be divined from the visible effects. Either leaving a will was against his principles or his hold over his children was so strong that he knew that he had no need to write his will down.

In 1656 occurred the family's first definitely recorded conviction for crime. Thomas Jarvis, labourer, was found guilty of breaking into the house of John Playle while nobody was at home at eleven in the morning and stealing £3 7s 1½d. The jury found it a true bill; he was sentenced and branded. It's a pity the record doesn't show his age or parentage to identify him by. There are two candidates: Thomas, the son of Thomas and Rebecca now Porter, aged twenty-seven, and Thomas, the son of Thomas and Mary Winterflood, aged fifteen.

I incline to the second, partly because it looks like a boy's crime, done on the spot because nobody was about, and because the one I think was the son of Thomas and Rebecca became a wheelwright, constable and man of some property.

At fifteen the other young Thomas was old enough to be employed by his father, Thomas senior, and therefore to be described as a labourer. His father was now forty-five and had buried one wife, Mary, and was to bury another two years after Thomas labourer's conviction. As well as Thomas they had had James and William, two attempts at a daughter Mary, and an Anne who had died at birth.

I get the impression that this branch of the family was hanging on economically by the skin of its teeth. Thomas the father died in 1683 and his freehold passed not to any of his children but to Abraham Jarvis, the son of Abraham the miller. What became of his sons is a mystery. Perhaps they moved away or were the forebears of some of the unidentifiable Jarvisses of surrounding villages.

The family was to have one more brush with the law before the Commonwealth was over. On the eve of the Restoration, in 1659, Abraham was summoned for sabbath-breaking, grinding corn on a Sunday. Fortunately for him such a crime was the business of the quarter sessions and Thaxted was currently in dispute with Chelmsford over its right as a borough to hold its own quarter sessions, a right that was upheld in 1660 when all indictments on the county files were discharged and no more were to be brought. Presumably when the town lost its charter under James II the right was also lost for good.

Meanwhile Abraham must have benefited by the dispute and if he was tried at all it would be at home in the Thaxted court house among relatives and friends where he could expect a lighter sentence. His offence is open to a couple of interpretations: either he was so far out on the dissenting wing as to disregard the sabbath or he was so little religious that it meant nothing to him, an unusual position for that time. Coupled with his failure to have his children baptised, apart from the eldest who was born right at the beginning of the Civil War, it certainly suggests that Abraham conformed only out of necessity. His brother Isaac had his children baptised, Isaac, Susan, Joseph and Grace, and so had Thomas and Sara who had brought their two namesakes to James Parkin as the country edged nearer to the Restoration. Abraham's brother Daniel had also brought his two sons to be christened Daniel in turn, before moving out to Bardfield where

he perhaps hoped his children would be stronger.

Cromwell died: 'men not much minding it.' Charles was brought in to the ringing of Thaxted bells. The church was swept and whitened and a new prayer book was bought. No doubt the boys came out to play 'cat' in the streets while their fathers slept in the chimney corners as Joslin saw in Colne, and maybe James Parkin 'went up and routed them' as he did. Christmas 1660 must have seen a return of the sports and pastimes that the radicals had tried so unsuccessfully to root out. Few people enjoying their Christmas ale and mince pies can have paused between mouthfuls to reflect that they heralded the return of the bishops and the ecclesiastical courts.

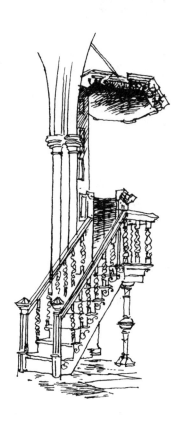

V   Green Mantles

James Parkin lost his job in 1662 along with some seventy other Essex ministers when the Act of Uniformity was enforced under which they had to declare publicly that it was unlawful to take up arms against the King, repudiate the Solemn League and Covenant, reaffirm the necessity of ordination by bishops and give 'unfeigned assent and consent to all and everything contained in the Book of Common Prayer'. Some had been sacked as soon as the King returned but Parkin had managed to hang on and even paid his hearth tax in 1662 for five hearths.

The tax shows five Jarvis households: Isaac, Abraham and Thomas senior were each rated at one; James at three and Thomas junior at four. One hundred and seventy families are listed, for the tax reached out to more people than ever before and was therefore even more hated. Sir Thomas Smith had eleven hearths and Robert Ffann seven. Then there was a group of six households with six, another group of six rated at five, and then a group of sixteen including Thomas junior with four. Women as well as men were included: ten widows and two who may have been spinsters. Below the tax threshold must lie another group, for Isaac and Abraham Jarvis, although only rated for one hearth or chimney, both described themselves as yeomen.

Some of the family were soon in trouble and summoned before the religious courts. Thomas Jarvis was fined and eventually excommunicated for not coming to common prayer at church on Sundays and holy days. Then James Jarvis and his son-in-law Thomas Drane were summoned with twenty-seven others for not taking communion. Daniel was fined for not attending church and so was either the husband or son of

Martha, Henry Badcock. Both Isaac and Thomas were excommunicated in 1665 for not bringing their children to be baptised.

The courts also concerned themselves with sexual morality. Robert Spilman was excommunicated for committing adultery with Sara, the wife of John Lawe the younger; Anna Mailer was under suspicion of incontinence with George Rushman; Robert Ffann and Mary Ellis were excommunicated for living together unmarried as man and wife; Elizabeth and Robert Knowles for co-habiting before marriage and having a child; John Everitt for living apart from his wife and keeping company with Widow Hastler, and John Smith for the 'common fame' of incontinence with Frances née Jarvis, the wife of Thomas Drane. One wonders whose unsavoury job it was to spy on the neighbours and lay these allegations before the courts; presumably the vicar and churchwardens'.

It can't, I think, be alleged that all these cases in one very small town were the result of the influence of a wicked and licentious royal court; for one thing they begin too soon after the Restoration. It seems more likely that the court, far from imitating the mores of French Louis, was actually reflecting the manners of the English countryside, and a new element of sexual freedom perhaps influenced by the radical wing of Puritanism including ranters and even to some extent Milton himself. It also seems a piece of incredible hypocrisy for society to have cracked down so hard on the sexual non-conformities of what must have been thousands of ordinary people, unless Thaxted was very atypical, while leaving those of great ones virtually untouched.

James Jarvis, whose daughter Frances was summoned in 1666, was a tailor of considerable wealth and property. He had been born a son of James in 1602. Frances was his second daughter and she was now thirty-eight and had married Thomas Drane, a blacksmith, some time before 1655 when James Parkin had registered their first daughter Frances. James's eldest daughter Ann, named after his mother, had married Thomas Warner in 1648. Mary had married Shadrack Andrews who kept The Axe, a vanished inn, and the other two girls, Priscilla and Jane, had married husbandmen from outside the town.

James himself had fallen in love with Tabitha, widow of Edward Lord alias Francis, and determined to marry her. One of

84

James's methods of providing for his daughters was to buy property from Mary's husband and then leave it to be sold and divided amongst the girls after his death. He also bought land from Tabitha Lord, and it was probably in the course of this that he decided to marry her, and indeed had the banns called before he made his will. He left her the inn at Mill End with the use of the brewery rent free for a year and a half after his death.

To Frances he left her husband's forge and another property in Mill End. After Frances died it was to be sold by James's executors if still living or, if not, by the vicar and churchwardens, and the money divided amongst her children. James, her eldest son, was to inherit the forge. To his youngest daughter Jane, only recently married, he left the handsome sum of £50; to his granddaughters by Priscilla amounts varying from £5 to £35. His favourite grandchild, also Priscilla, got the furniture in his best chamber as well, his daughter Jane got that in the parlour, while Mary had his sideboard and table. The Warner grandchildren weren't forgotten either.

By any standards James Jarvis had done well. At the quarter sessions in 1661 the annual rate for an employed tailor was fifty shillings plus ten shillings' livery, so what James left to his daughter Jane alone represented over sixteen years' wages for a man in his trade. I have tried to see how he could have made so much money in such a small town but there's no clue. The provision of coats for the Commonwealth soldiers, which would have been an explanation, went, like the provision of arms and saddles, to a London merchant. Nor can I discover whether James could read and write. Presumably he could measure well enough to fit his customers and he seems to have been good at counting his money.

Both James and his son-in-law Drane had put up a token resistance to the re-Established Church and had then conformed. Isaac's crime was greater and also more surprising since he had had his previous children baptised. Perhaps he objected to the replacement of James Parkin. But the real non-conformist was Thomas. It's clear that his wasn't a moment's obstinacy but a constantly held course and I believe he is the one who appears in Besse's *Book of Sufferings of the People Called Quakers* as arrested in 1670 and fined, with William Osborn and Thomas Johnson, for attending a Quaker meeting, although his name doesn't appear among the scanty Quaker register entries.

In a rate of 1662, Thomas Jarvis senior and junior are both listed under Richmond's Green and Monk Street, where there was a house belonging to Edwin Morrell where Quaker meetings were held, and a burial ground whose records are unfortunately very incomplete. Morrell appears higher up in a list of those fined in Besse's book and he is down as paying a total of £51 10s 0d at various times for being caught at meetings, often in his own house.

The original Quakers were, as their name implies, anything but calm and quiet people. Ralph Joslin was frankly frightened of them because of their unpredictable and enthusiastic behaviour. 'Great noise of people called Quakers; divers have fits about us and are thereby come to be able to speak; the Lord help us to stand fast against every evil and error . . . Heard and true that Turner's daughter was distract in this quaking business; sad are the fits at Coxall [Coggeshall] like the pow wowing among the Indies. Heard this morning that James Parnel the father of the Quakers in these parts having undertaken to fast forty days and nights was, die ten, in the morning found dead . . . It's said in the country that his party went to Colchester to see his resurrection again . . . A quaker wench came boisterously into the church up almost to the desk, I perceived persons expected some disturbance but she stayed the end and then went out quietly, blessed be God.'

The Quakers were numerous and determined in Thaxted, and in 1670 thirteen of them were excommunicated. The penalty for excommunication could be imprisonment in Colchester gaol where plague or gaol fever might carry you off.

There was another group of dissidents in Thaxted too, of the older Puritans who were to form the basis of the later non-conformist sects, and several of these were summoned the same year for attending private conventicles and collecting money for those who unlawfully taught at the meetings. At the same time James Parkin was arrested for being such a teacher. Not surprisingly, among the names appear some who had been prominent in the Commonwealth: John Humphrey, who had been a witness for the sequestrators, was fined for not contributing to the minister's dues; Francis Bowtell, a tax collector in Oliver's day, for forsaking the church and William Turner, a relative of Captain Richard the sequestrator, for not paying dues and for not paying for the breaking of the ground in the churchyard to bury his mother.

Not paying towards the minister was indeed a form of passive resistance, but in some cases the crime the courts dealt with could be described as simple compassion. The Widow Barber was summoned for sheltering a pregnant woman and refusing to reveal the name of the father of the illegitimate child. This must have been following a complaint of the churchwardens who were afraid the child would become a charge on the parish if it couldn't be laid to the charge of the father. Parishes had a duty to provide for their old, sick, orphaned and indigent, so there was much competition to make sure that the responsibility was really theirs and couldn't be deposited elsewhere. Pregnant unmarried women were often given money to move on to another parish if they weren't locals so that the child should be born within someone else's area of responsibility.

Crimes or their prosecution had fashions. 1670 was the year for the crackdown on religious non-conformity, though it included two occasions when women hadn't come to give thanks at the church after childbirth and one instance of the most popular offence in 1668: 'committing fornication together or living incontinently together before marriage.' Among the five cases were Andrew Jarvis, son of Abraham the miller, and Helen Smith. Andrew and Helen were finally married on April 15, 1667 and their son Andrew was baptised on the 16th.

The phrase 'living incontinently together' suggests that these weren't cases of pre-marital sex, fornication, but actual cohabiting. Presumably a contract had been made between the couple and their respective parents settling the marriage portion, even if only orally, but they had felt no need of the church's blessing until the first child was about to be declared a bastard with all the difficulties and disabilities that would follow. At least one branch of the Smiths was Quaker but it's impossible to tell whether Helen belonged to this branch and if there was a religious element in her late marriage, because there's no record of her baptism to show who her parents were.

Among the lesser gentry, including the clergy, there was still a strong element of arrangement in marriages, although it's clear from Ralph Joslin's accounts of his daughter's toings and froings that the girl had the last word. This wasn't always the case where a large estate was involved. Among the yeomen the girl still brought some portion with her. Thomas Jarvis of Duck End, son of Abraham's brother Daniel, in his will as late as 1719 speaks of things his wife brought with her on marriage and the girl was still expected to produce that bottom drawer of needlework that has only disappeared since the Second World War. One of Joslin's daughters carried forty pounds' worth of work and plate with her and yeomen's wives provided those household goods now usually supplied as wedding presents including the invaluable porridge pot. In my childhood the two staple items were the canteen of cutlery and the dinner service that when a few pieces had been broken at festive family gatherings came down to provide the plates and gravy boat for Sunday dinner after a Sunday morning walk to the pub.

The royal court and the balladeers were well aware of the comparatively uninhibited sex life of the countryside, uninhibited that is until brought to the notice of the church courts and quarter sessions, which also concerned themselves with bastardy but on a practical, not a moral, level of who was to pay for the child's support. The mother could be sent into service or to the house of correction where the inmates worked to keep themselves.

The attitude of the court as reflected in the ballads and theatre songs was largely one of disguised envy that veered between the romanticism of *The Happy Husbandman* and the coarse realism of *A Ballad of Andrew and Maudlin*.

> My young Mary do's mind the dairy,
> While I go a howing and mowing each morn;
> Then hey the little spinning-wheel
> Merrily round do's reel
>   while I am singing amidst the corn:
> Cream and kisses both are my delight
> She gives me them, and the joys of night;
> She's soft as the air, as morning fair
> Is not such a maid a most pleasing sight?

sings the happy husbandman, like Andrew Jarvis, with a determination to 'observe the lives our fathers led'. He will live without ambition and sedition, those two late destroyers of the settled order, 'And leave state affairs to the state-man's head' as he sleeps under his thatch with a quilt of roses. The ballad is being used to tell him how good his life is compared with the lives of the great or the city-dweller.

At the same time, in songs for their own consumption, the court pointed up the difference between themselves and the country people who could nevertheless be used as images for their own sexual adventures suitably polished in the pastoral.

Andrew chuck'd Maudlin under the chin,
   Simper she did like a furmity kettle;
The twang of whose blubber lips made such a din,
   As if her chaps had been made of bell-metal:
Kate laughed heartily at the same smack,
And loud she did answer it with a bum-crack.

Here they did fling, and there they did hoist,
   Here a hot breath, and there went a savour;
Here they did glance, and there they did gloist,
   Here they did simper, and there they did slaver;
Here was a hand, and there was a placket,
Whilst, hey! their sleeves went flicket-a flacket.

The dance being ended, they sweat and they stunk,
   The maidens did smirk it, the youngsters did kiss 'em,
Cakes and ale flew about, they clapp'd hands and drunk;
   They laugh'd and they giggl'd until they bepist 'em;
They laid the girls down, and gave each a green mantle,
While their breasts and their bellies went pintle a pantle.

The green mantle was formed from the grass stains on the backs and shoulders of the girls' gowns as they were pressed back in the long grass. Ironically there was often greater privacy and comfort for making love in the open air than in an overcrowded house where you shared a bed or lay on a hard pallet.

The preferred fare of the country people themselves was the kind of true life love adventure, often told with great charm, of the 'Come all ye's and the 'As I walked out's that Tom Durfey gathered, embroidered and invented in his *Pills To Purge Melancholy* and that was still being sung at the beginning of this century in Essex farmhouses.

As I walked out one fine morning,
One midsummer morning so early,
I found a fair maid by my way.
I says, 'Are you young Mary?'

Such a song would be fined down by successive singers, purged of any political overtones except those of country versus town, and any suggestion of country coarseness, until it could tell an unencumbered tale that might nevertheless carry a warning at the end on the probable consequences of girls having sexual affairs before marriage. The freshness of country girls was often praised and their freedom from both the pox and the scars of smallpox that the immunity of their dairy work with its doses of cow pox often gave them.

The case of Frances Drane, née Jarvis, the daughter of James the tailor who was accused of incontinence with John Smith which I've mentioned earlier was, however, a strange one. The accused couple were excommunicated but Thomas Drane himself went to court and asked that the penalty should be lifted from his wife until she could come herself and explain. Her explanation hasn't survived and so can only be guessed at.

She was no green girl at thirty-eight. Apart from a daughter Frances, she and Thomas had had four sons, the last born in 1661. Then in 1664 she had another boy who was christened John, an earlier John having died. But John was also the name of her supposed lover and it was perhaps this and the possibility that he was one of the Quaker Smiths that had given rise to the gossip.

Much sarcastic play was made with Quaker doctrines of love and brotherhood being only a cover for fornication, and scurrilous ballads on this theme circulated freely. A John Smith had married an Anna Knowles in 1634 and many of the Knowles family were certainly Quakers, appearing in their registers and among a group from Thaxted who were taken at a meeting in 1661 and imprisoned for three months for refusing to take the oath.

In spite of their numbers the Quakers in Thaxted had a rough time until the 1672 amnesty by Charles II, which, however, parliament soon rescinded although three thousand licences had been issued for independent meeting houses which seem to have been allowed to continue. But even after this in 1684 a Colonel Turner with a band of others locked up the Quaker meeting house one night to prevent them using it and then in the morning unlocked it and took out all the benches and furniture and burned them on the green. Was this Richard the sequestrator become conformist? His sister had married the vicar Robert Barnard so perhaps it was. He seems however to have been promoted, though I've been unable to find any appropriate Colonel Turner in the army lists of the time; however one had been active earlier, according to Besse, when soldiers were brought in to deal with the Quakers, often beating them up brutally.

Thaxted escaped the great plague; at least the burial register shows none of that horrifying increase that makes city registers such tragic documents. No doubt the inhabitants watched its approach to Colchester, where it raged among the poor, and to Braintree and Coggeshall with the same mixture of fear and fascination that moved Ralph Joslin as he saw 'sinful Colne', as he called it, spared. But the events of a hundred years before when the sweating sickness carried off Margaret Jarvis weren't repeated.

Indeed Thaxted seemed a healthy place for those who managed to grow up. Thomas's children Abraham, Isaac and Daniel were in their sixties and seventies by the end of Charles II's reign, though there is no record that any of them repeated their father's septuagenarian feat. Prices had fallen although rents had risen, and they must have been able to eat well from their own produce and have some over to sell, so that they could buy or lease more land and supplement their own food with a few luxuries like the new green peas Joslin had first recorded eating during the Commonwealth.

In spite of the remaining religious troubles and the conflict with James II, in which Thaxted lost its charter, more I suspect from an unwillingness than an inability to pay, and became a borough only in name, there is a pastoral Golden Age quality about the last years of the seventeenth century. Men and women worked hard, the women not only keeping the dairy and the poultry but making jams, wines, medicines and what would now be labelled toiletries, soaps, rose and lavender water, and spinning in their spare moments for sale as well as home use. Children too span and worked in field or farm, minding the herds or scaring the birds. Men worked in the fields and often had a trade as well. There was variety of job, companionship and often of scene as people went into town to shop, visited relatives or went to the city for jury service, to vote or to draw up a lease. There were fairs, church ales and a round of seasonal festivals to look forward to, so that life wasn't all work. The weather itself could be relied on to give an extra holiday from time to time and winter to slacken the pace of life.

Not everyone enjoyed this relatively comfortable standard of living but it did stretch further down the social scale than it was to reach again until the late twentieth century as the hundreds of wills from the period testify. Abraham, Isaac and Daniel were all freeholders and yeomen though they none of them seem to have voted in the 1679 election. In the hearth tax of eight years before, Daniel now living in Lindsell was rated for three, Abraham for one, his son Andrew for two and Thomas Jarvis junior for four chimneys. Thomas senior was rated at one on which the taxman had been unable to collect.

Andrew wasn't a yeoman but a husbandman and he shared his house with his brother Thomas, a cordwainer. There were now three Thomas Jarvisses again: the cordwainer, Thomas wheelwright and plain Thomas. The wheelwright seems to be the son of Rebecca, now Widow Porter, for in his son's will part of bewitched James's property called Soules appears. The last Thomas was the son of Joseph and brother of that Mary who had run off with Thomas Saggers and forfeited her inheritance. Daniel also had a son Thomas, known as 'of Duck End', Lindsell.

In 1669 a Thomas was chosen constable, presumably Thomas wheelwright of the four hearths, who was still doing the job at the end of the century. He can't, I think, have been the Quaker since he would have been caught in a clash of loyalties and might anyway have been ineligible under the Corporation Act.

It looks, however, as if most of the family had abandoned the Church of England. Only Andrew and Helen had their children baptised in the parish church, and after their marriage there's only one Jarvis marriage until the wedding of their son Andrew nearly twenty years later. Thomas, the son of Joseph, and husband of Sarah, had two of his children baptised before the

Restoration but not the others, of whom at least three survived to be mentioned in his will. Nor is there any record of his burial around 1690. He is, however, top of the list in 1683 of those not coming to the Sacrament, together with his wife.

He had done well, buying Sibleys from Henry Eve which he left to his son Joseph, and the Hill, which was occupied by John Dunmow, one of the leading spirits among the early non-conformists, which he left to his son Thomas. One of his daughters had married Daniel Gun whose family for many years followed the, to us, exotic sounding trade of fanwright though I suspect that they were winnowing fans not ones simply for cooling hot foreheads. Thomas's three daughters were to get £20 apiece. His wife seems to have been already dead.

Abraham the miller had died in 1680. He left Dawnes Mill to his eldest son Abraham after the death of his mother, 'Mary my loving wife'. She was to enjoy all his property 'with all the orchard and two pightles of land'. After her death their second son Andrew was to have £6, Thomas, the third son, was to have the pightle of one acre and their grandchildren by Andrew were to have five shillings each.

The younger Abraham died a single man, as the register rather tartly records, ten years after his father, and a conflict then arose between Mary his mother and his brother Thomas over his property. The court first upheld Thomas's claim and then revoked it in her favour. Mary never forgave him and cut him out of her own will with the proverbial shilling, leaving all her movable goods to Andrew when she died two years later. Andrew had also inherited his uncle's, her brother John Overall's, property after his well-beloved wife's death. Presumably they were childless. Overall had left Abraham his nephew, who was still alive when he made his will, £5 and Andrew £10. The house and lands were to go first to Mary Overall and then to Andrew or his son Thomas. The other Thomas was completely left out. John Overall like his brother-in-law, Abraham Jarvis, was a yeoman. A previous John seems from his will to have been a carpenter as well. Thomas cordwainer must have fallen out with his mother before the probate dispute; either that or he was generally disliked in the family, for her brother to leave him out of his will too.

Isaac also cut one of his children, Joseph, off with a shilling when he made his will in 1693, but I have been unable to find out why, though a Joseph Jarvis was one of the overseers of the poor at the parish church at about this time so perhaps they had disagreed over religion. Isaac had two more sons, Daniel and William, who were to be paid £20 each by instalments of £5 a year after the death of Isaac's wife Susanna. Payment was to be made by his son Andrew in the south porch of the parish church in return for Andrew's inheriting an orchard meadow called Poorerood 'with the apples'.

Two married daughters were each to receive £14 and the manner of their payment may reflect either their characters or their circumstances, for Susanna, wife of Robert Warner wheelwright, was to have hers as twenty shillings a year while Grace, wife of Jonathan Savill of no stated occupation, was to have hers in two equal lumps. Isaac the eldest son was to have 'the messuage where I now dwell'.

It's interesting that at this time a man could make his will disposing of his property after his wife's death and she, either by custom or law, seemingly had no power to alter that. Even Mary, Abraham's widow, was only able to dispose of her own small goods to Andrew in her rage against Thomas. When she died the manor court recorded the inheritance of the lands roughly according to Abraham's will though the larger part went now to Andrew as the elder son. What isn't clear is what precisely of her son Abraham's property Mary had disputed with Thomas.

Isaac's sons had mostly moved away from Thaxted. Isaac junior had gone to Debden, where he was a churchwarden, but he sent back the bodies of his children, both named Andrew, to be buried in Thaxted, and then that of his wife Rachel, followed four years later by his own. He left two sons: Isaac who moved up into Suffolk and William who disappears from the records unless he is the one buried in Thaxted in the middle of the eighteenth century. Isaac junior's will is very like those of a century and a half before, with its bequests of a bed, hutches, stools, a little table, the great mashing tub, the trunk in the parlour and 'all my linen and pewter equally divided'. Lifestyle changed very little as reflected in its furnishings.

He had bidden his sons look after his mother and see that she 'wanted for no necessaries'. Susanna née Purchas was a tough old bird who had outlasted her husband by over a quarter of a century and now saw out her eldest son.

The first of the brothers to die had been Daniel, buried in woollen at Great Bardfield in 1679. The woollen shroud was by Act of Parliament in an attempt to promote the wool trade, and much resented. The year before his death there had been great excitement in the neighbourhood when the Scottish troops of the Earl of Dumbarton had been stationed there on their way home from France, Captain Melville's troop being sent to Thaxted, and they probably behaved much as soldiers tend to do on demob. However there can't have been a great deal they could teach the locals in such matters for a few years after Daniel's death his son Thomas was involved in one of the family's more unsavoury episodes, when Mary, wife of William How, accused Thomas of 'having knowledge' of her and he was admitted to prison. I can only assume that this was a case of some form of alleged rape.

As his surety at the hearing he had his brother-in-law Richard Juniper. Whether Thomas was guilty or not, his family stood by him or at least his sister Mary Juniper did, for she left him £5 in her will. She and Richard had no children of their own, so most of their property was divided between their nephews and nieces among whom were Thomas's children and those of his other sisters. The families were all very close. Thomas Jarvis witnessed a will with Richard Juniper and Richard Turner, and the Turners, father and son, witnessed Juniper's will, in which he left his property at Richmond Green to his wife.

Thomas must have settled down after his unconventional beginning. Seven years later he married Margaret Hawkes who was probably a relative by marriage since his sister had married Zachary Hawkes. In his will she is his 'loving wife'. Once again as in other branches of the family, there are no baptismal records for his seven children. He married either late in life or twice for Margaret outlived him by many years. It wasn't only the men who reached ripe old age. Provided a woman was childless or strong enough to cope with constant childbirth she too might survive into her seventies or eighties if she belonged to the yeoman class and was able to eat, clothe and warm herself well.

But to carry this out needed constant labour and attention to detail. All the basic foods, bread, butter, cheese, beer, that were made at home, needed a long and many-staged process from the raw materials if they were to be nutritious and above all palatable.

One mistake in the making and the week's bread would be mouldy, the cheese sour or the beer off. When it came to salting and curing, making sausages and brawn, it could be a whole year's produce at stake.

And for most women the knowledge of the processes that now occupy a dozen industries with their chemists, technicians and engineers had to be held in their heads, for, if the men were illiterate, so, more so if that's possible, were their wives. Everything had to be remembered and all measures were by eye, by feel or by accepted practices and the approved bushel container. Where foods were commercially made, largely for the consumption of the poorer people who were unable to run a totally self-sufficient home-based economy, their production was overseen by the local weights and measures officers, the ale conners and bread weighers, who were elected annually at the manor courts like the constables and leather sealers.

The latest modern methods of teaching the first steps in mathematics by measuring instead of by sums on a page are a reversion to pre-numeracy, a recognition of the practical as a legitimate stage on the way. Abraham the miller must have conducted his business by these methods. The unground wheat had to produce a recognised amount of flour, and both were measured not by weight but by container. Joseph the overseer of the poor, who attended to the practical side of the disbursements, signed his accounts with a cross although his fellow overseers could write their names. Richard Juniper and Thomas Jarvis also made their marks as witnesses to a will. The voting procedure for the Knights of the Shire recognised that many of the gentlemen freeholders, as they were called, would be unlettered. To vote you raised a hand and shouted, gave your voice, much as in many factory meetings today. The secret ballot only becomes possible when enough people can read and write and disenfranchises those who can't, unless recognisable visual symbols can be found as hieroglyphs. Whig could have been shown quite simply but Tory would have been more difficult to devise a symbol for.

The running of the intricate home economy depended on the wife being fit and intelligent in a practical way. Ironically, if she was suffering from malnutrition, with the apathy and inability to concentrate that it brings, she would be unable to make the right steps to restore herself and her family. Once the cycle of being well-fed was broken it was very difficult to restore. The temptation to sit by the fire instead of going briskly to the cold dairy to take the cheese out of the press, take off its damp cloth, wrap it in a dry one and re-weight it in the press, a process that had to be repeated every two hours for a day as the second stage of the cheese-making, was physiologically irresistible to the already half-starved, and undernourishment accounted for a great deal of the indolence noted by writers on the poor and preachers to them, particularly the women who had no master on their backs except the one who came home tired at night to a thin supper and their unsatisfied grizzling children.

This is now recognised as a simple biological fact, countered in some cases by an enormous will to survive that could produce superhuman, in the strictest sense, efforts. But, not knowing this in any scientific way, the responsible authorities of earlier generations were forced to employ what means they had from the proto-sciences of theology, politics, ethics to try to understand a situation and remedy it, a situation that was to worsen rapidly from that late seventeenth-century heyday. Their methods were mainly to juggle with the poor laws and the price of corn.

Old age may have prevented several of the brothers Daniel, Isaac and Abraham from voting in the 1679 election but it doesn't explain the absence of Thomas. To vote meant a journey to Chelmsford along twenty miles of bad roads, but four of the family made it in 1694 and in February too when ways were notoriously foul: 'February fill the dyke, be it black or be it white,' as Maud learned to say.

The election was caused by the suicide of John Lemott Honeywood, who became melancholic after his wife had tricked him into settling all his estate on her by frightening him with the imminent return of King James who would confiscate all his property. After two attempts to stifle himself, once by thrusting the rump of a turkey down his throat and again by trying to swallow tobacco-pipe ends, and then trying to throw himself downstairs, he lured his attendant away by sending him to fetch a glass of small beer and hanged himself from the curtain rod of his bed with a broken garter.

The 'gentlemen' of the county put up Sir Charles Barrington as candidate while 'the factious party' put up Benjamin Mildmay.

The Jarvisses voted en masse for Mildmay, the family providing twenty per cent of his Thaxted votes. Several of those who voted with them had appeared before the ecclesiastical courts on various charges of non-conformity.

Twice as many voted for Sir Charles Barrington who was elected, including old Presbyterians and royalists now joined in the new establishment: Richard Turner and his vicar brother-in-law Robert Barnard, Nat Westley, John Humphrey and Henry Leader, while among the voters for Barrington in Great Dunmow a few miles away was Henry Gilder.

VI   *The Saracen's Head*

Lydia's ancestor Henry Gilder first appears, seemingly from nowhere, as the landlord owner of the Saracen's Head, the handsome old coaching inn in the middle of Great Dunmow. He wasn't there in 1671 to pay his hearth tax but by 1686 he was appearing at the Quarter Sessions in a bastardy case, where it isn't clear whether he is one of the complaining overseers or supporting the father of the child, Samuel Voice.

The year before, his own daughter Priscilla had been baptised, the first of his children to show up in the Great Dunmow registers. His wife was called Elizabeth and in the following years they had Mary, Thomas, Grace who survived only a brief time, William, Anne, Susannah, Jane, and Robert and Henry who were baptised elsewhere.

There had been Gilders in the area for some time. John and Mary had had a string of children at Little Easton beginning in the 1670s but I've found no traceable connection between the families. They were summoned in 1683 for refusing to come to the sacrament, like Thomas Jarvis of Sibley's Green and Thomas of Lindsell, so presumably they too were non-conformist.

The Saracen's Head was a thriving business, popular for the dinners that topped off every piece of committee work, and for civic occasions. Its owner could make a very good living indeed but he could leave it to only one of his children and Henry Gilder chose his, presumably eldest, son Henry who was described in 1714 as junior on the baptism of his and his wife Frances's daughter Ann.

Whether they fell out with their father over his disposal of the inn or merely felt that the town had enough Gilders, Henry's other sons left Great Dunmow. Thomas went to Widen in Hertfordshire and became a gardener; William went to Thaxted, to be followed later by Robert. Both William and Thomas called one of their sons Henry and the name continued in the family down to the mid-twentieth century.

William married Elizabeth Wyatt, daughter of a farmer John, in 1714. For some reason they were married by licence, perhaps because she was already pregnant, and not in Great Dunmow but in Thundridge where his brother Thomas was living with his wife Jane. Thomas was one witness and a mysterious George Gilder, farmer of Dunmow, a brother or close relative, was the other. The couple returned to Dunmow, where their first child was baptised Elizabeth, followed by William the next year and then Henry. They must have moved to Thaxted in the next couple of years for Mary was baptised there in 1719, the first Gilder to appear in the Thaxted registers. Five more children followed.

The year before William's marriage a common scandal had overtaken the family. His eldest sister Susan had been seduced and become pregnant by a doctor called Thomas Finch from Much Hadham in Hertfordshire. Either he was staying at the Saracen's Head, which seems the likelier, or he was attending the family professionally.

Finch must have been either the elder, aged about fifty-six, or his son aged thirty-five. Susan Gilder was eighteen. Their son Thomas was registered under his mother's name as 'base born'. The father was hailed before the quarter sessions before the baby's birth for getting the mother 'with a bastard child which is likely to be chargeable to the parish where it is born'. He was released, presumably after agreeing to be responsible for the child's maintenance.

Thomas Finch the elder had married Ann Summers in 1676. Five years later, and described as barber, he had been summoned with some others for poaching a buck with greyhounds in the park belonging to Walter, Lord Aston, at Standon. In 1709 he received his certificate from the College of Physicians as 'well qualified to practise physick'. His wife died in 1726 and Thomas himself, 'an old man', in 1736. He doesn't mention any sons in his will, only daughters and their husbands and children. Most of his property, including his house, he leaves to his unmarried daughter Anne, now over fifty, who had no doubt been the one to be left at home to look after ageing parents, often the lot of the youngest. His daughter Sarah had married John Want, a bricklayer, who had been Thomas Finch's surety in the bastardy trial. I can find no evidence that Thomas junior was a physician as well as his father and therefore have to conclude that Thomas senior was the begetter of Susan Gilder's child, who, along with his mother, passes out of sight as bastards so often seemed to do. Their mothers often remained:

To live dishonoured and to die unwed
For clowns grow jealous when they're once misled.

William Gilder bought himself a farm called Mill Hill and in 1719 he and Robert Jarvis were elected constables, the first official coming together of Samuel and Lydia's ancestors.

Robert Jarvis had been elected first in 1707 and then again in 1719 but hadn't turned up at the manor court to be sworn and was therefore remanded to the quarter sessions for swearing in, where there was no escape. Robert was the son of Andrew who had died in 1705. In many ways Andrew represents the zenith in Jarvis fortunes, for in 1683 he had leased the farm and house called Armigers that guards the entrance to the long drive to Horham Hall itself and is now a handsome pink-washed building. With it went one hundred and eight acres, two closes of glebe land, one called Wildnett field of twenty acres and another called Milcroft of six, a grove, spring or wood of three acres, four acres of pasture called Botlers and five acres in Common Mead, mostly lying between Horham Park gate and Cutlers Green. The original lease for eight years was renewed in 1697 and the property was to go on Andrew's death to his son Thomas and his daughters Mary, Martha and Sara. The rent was originally £36 a year but when Thomas inherited in 1704 it had risen to £80.

Andrew's other son Robert inherited his grandfather Abraham's mill but he doesn't seem to have been a miller himself. The building was still called Millhouse but he seems to have been a farmer. This was a pity for a miller could make a good living, as Abraham had done. It seems unlikely that Robert simply gave up a thriving business passed on by his father. It must surely be that the river which drove the mill changed course or fell in volume or that there was a shift from arable to pasture or that there was pressure on tenants to use the manor mill at Horham Hall. The second suggestion isn't borne out by developments in the county as a whole, which was turning more and more to grain production as the London population, and therefore market, grew.

Andrew, Robert's father, had supplied wood to the parish overseers in the winter of 1698 to give to the poor 'in the cold time'. He had also served his time as overseer in 1704 and signed his name to the annual accounts. To be able to sign one's name doesn't necessarily imply full literacy but Andrew's is a good firm signature with the letters well formed, in contrast with Robert's scratchy and uncertain one, and better even than that of a Thomas Jarvis who begins to put his name to accounts ten years later, 'With learning just enough to sign a name' as Clare was to observe.

Thomas Jarvis wheelwright, as he was known, had been elected constable for several years in the nineties and had twice been summoned to the Quarter Sessions, once as a guilty, once as an injured party. The first time he was fined for 'carelessly letting go' a poacher, Robert Howlet, who had been arrested for coursing or killing deer in Lord Maynard's park, put in Thaxted gaol, broke prison, was caught next day but 'let go' before he reached the county gaol. For this Thomas was fined two shillings, the court perhaps suspecting collusion.

The second time he had his prisoner taken from him by John Lord, tailor, who was summoned for 'refusing to aid him, for abusing him and rescuing one Browne'. The constable's lot was sometimes not a happy one.

It wasn't, I think, this Thomas but Andrew's eldest son who fathered an illegitimate son in 1695. The mother was an oddly named friend of the family, Abigail Jealous, who had witnessed his great uncle John Overall's will while Thomas Jealous witnessed his grandmother Mary's. The child was baptised at Broxted, a little parish neighbouring Thaxted, into which part of Andrew's lands at Armigers may have stretched or indeed the farm and eighteen acres called Sawers which Thomas had inherited via his father from John Overall. Rather unusually, the child, who was christened Andrew, was given his father's surname and, perhaps because of it, did a little better than bastards usually did, growing up to marry and father a child himself although he died the following year at only thirty-six.

Towards the end of the seventeenth century Thaxted began to have a woman from time to time as an overseer, always of course a widow. Women barely had names of their own in any practical sense. They were mostly referred to as someone's daughter, wife or widow. Thomas Drane's wife Judith was the sister of Lawrence Porter. Thomas himself was the eldest child of Frances, the daughter of James Jarvis who had been excommunicated earlier in the century. His wife may have been a midwife. Like the Dame Dorothy of the folk play *St George and the Turkish Knight*, she was a healer and frequently employed by the overseers to treat poor patients whom they paid her for. It would be interesting to know what her success rate was compared with that of the various doctors the parish also employed whose fees were much higher than Goody Drane's.

Medicine was still in its humours phase with great emphasis on purging and bleeding. Even infants a few days old would be bled. Standards varied enormously. The Chelmsford bonesetter called Strut, for example, was clearly incompetent and after four tries at setting a shoulder was forced to send for his master from Bishop's Stortford. Sir John Bramston records the final happy operation on his son. 'So he consented they should try, and they laid him on his back, and himself took a towel and put under the armhole, but upon a bolster, and put the other end of the towel about his own neck, being a very strong man; and three men holding my son by the other arm and his legs, and all pulling hard at once, Strut with his foot, put in the bone into its place which gave a snap that all heard it; and my son endured it with great patience and courage, after four fruitless attempts; for which God be praised.'

In 1710 the parish paid Dr Chapman's bill of £3 . 18s . 6d for attending Thomas Jarvis in his sickness. Chapman was not successful. The Parish also paid £1 . 6s . 3d to Thomas's family, 14s . 4d for a coffin, a shroud and 'laying him forth', and 2s . 0d for the grave and knell. It then bought a spinning wheel for widow Jarvis to help support herself and her family, costing 2s . 6d. Thomas was buried as 'pater-familias'. I think he was the one who had married Ann Browne of Great Easton in 1697 and had had several children, including the first recorded twins in the family, but I'm not at all sure which branch he belonged to except that it was one which had slipped badly. Perhaps he was buried in the evening as the custom sometimes was so that the dead went to their last rest when the living were going to their beds.

Had Joseph Jarvis been alive to see the results of the runaway marriage of his daughter Mary with Thomas Saggers, he could have said 'I told you so' with some justification for they were in deep trouble. Her husband, as I've said, had died in 1693, leaving her with Joseph, her handicapped son, to look after but her other two sons, now middle-aged, were either unlucky or improvident and a constant charge on the parish.

Allowed Thomas Saggers when he was turned out of house and his wife was sick	2s . 4d
Thomas Saggers being lame	6s . 4d
Thomas Saggers wife the time of her lying in	7s . 6d
For a coffin for Saggers child	

And so the entries go on, with shoes for 'Saggers boy', hose for 'Saggers girl', money for the girl when she was sick, 'a pair of leather britches' for one boy and so forth – painting a picture of almost total dependence on the parish. At times it's impossible to tell which of Mary's sons is meant, though it seems to have been Robert's children who were finally taken into care and numbered among the fifty people in receipt of weekly assistance. Both Joseph and Thomas Saggers, and the widow of Thomas Jarvis, were on this list in 1711, receiving 6s a month 'out of the house', for Thaxted had set up its own workhouse in June of that year to accommodate some of its poor, although the same number continued to be supported outside. There are payments to workmen for removing the poor's goods to the House. Anyone's chattels in the road waiting for the van look pathetic enough but these must have been a truly pitiful collection, though the authorities must be given something for having the imagination to let the inmates bring some of their own things with them to that place 'not contrived for want to live, but die'.

At least in this local workhouse they ate well, the purchases including wheat for bread, malt and hops for beer as well as beer itself, beans, cheese, butter, oatmeal, beef, lamb, milk, pepper, salt and sugar and tobacco.

But however good the provisions, the House, as it was called in Essex, was feared and hated. Even as late as the beginning of our century people prayed to 'be took' rather than go there. Clare in his portrait of his parish workhouse fifty miles from Thaxted says that it had no windows, 'a luxury deemed to pride's disdainful eye'. Prices had been high at the end of the seventeenth century, wheat, the standard measure, rising to 9s . 8d the bushel, but by 1713 the workhouse was paying only 5s. Wages were now about 8s a week for a labourer. Women's shoes were from 2s . 6d to 3s, men's 3s . 6d to 4s; a woman's gown cost 6s . 9d, a man's trousers 4s 6d while a man's coat with a pair of linings against the winter cold cost 11s . 4d. A shift, the basic undergarment, for a child cost 1s . 2d and a handkerchief was a shilling. A coat then cost a week and a half's wage where now it costs half a week's; a pair of men's shoes half a week where now they are less than a tenth. In 1720, when Andrew Jarvis fell sick, his monthly rate for assistance was 7s . 4d.

I think this Andrew was a son of Isaac fallen on hard times because of sickness. The parish had paid his year's rent of £1 . 10s . 0d in 1710 and then no more until his last illness ten years later. Both he and his wife were ill. She recovered and the parish paid the rent for her the following year. In spite of parish relief Andrew wasn't buried in the parish church. He had married a girl called Ann, as so many of the Jarvis wives were at this time, presumably after the princess as she must have been when the girls were born. One of their many children was called Isaac, which makes me think this may have been a descendant of his. On the other hand Isaac had left his son Andrew to pay the considerable sums of £20 each to two of his brothers in return for inheriting the orchard, which doesn't suggest a poor man, so it may be that this Andrew is the only recorded child born in 1667 of a mysterious couple Andrew and Elizabeth.

Many of the family had still not conformed to the Established Church and so their ramifications were hard to sort out. An independent chapel had been licensed in 1672 by John Reynolds, and by 1716 when John Shute Barrington wrote about it to Dr Evans who was collecting information on Non-conformity, he estimated that it had a congregation of five hundred, including twenty voters and four 'gentlemen'. Its records for the early period haven't survived but among them must have been many Jarvis entries. Thomas of Lindsell was arrested at the beginning of the century and hailed to Dunmow Archdeaconry Court for not paying his rates. The following year shows charges for the churchwarden going to Dunmow for the court and refreshing himself at Henry Gilder's Saracen's Head. Sometimes there were late conformities: James Jarvis 'an adult' was baptised in the parish church in 1718 and nearly forty years later Joseph 'upwards of seventy years of age'.

In 1710 there was an election at which five of the Jarvisses voted in Thaxted and two Henry Gilders, father and son, voted in Great Dunmow. This time, instead of a Jarvis block vote for the Whig candidates, they were split. Two Thomases and a Joseph voted for the Whigs, Thomas Middleton and Sir Francis Masham, while another Thomas and Robert voted Tory for Sir Richard Child. The Gilders voted for Child too. Five years later the voting was the same as far as party was concerned, although the candidates had changed, except that Whig Joseph Jarvis was absent. He died in 1718, or at least his will was proved then though there's no recorded burial in the parish church, but he had made his will in 1713 and may therefore have been too ill to vote.

He left all his considerable property to his wife Sara with the unfortunate caveat now creeping into Jarvis wills: 'she keeping herself a widow.' After her death or remarriage, Sibleys Green, his main property, with twenty acres 'more or less', was to go to son William who married Deborah Green and moved to Stebbing, thus renewing a branch of the family there, and bequeathing Sibleys to his son William in 1735. Joseph in his will made provision for William to pay three pounds yearly to son Joseph, which suggests that he may have been in some way unable to earn a living.

Joseph also had two other sons, Thomas, who must have been one of the other Whig voters, and received three crofts amounting to twenty-seven acres which belonged to the small manor of Priors Hall, and the mysterious Daniel, who got two pieces of land making three and a half acres. There was also son James, who got two fields, and four daughters, who were to receive ten

108

pounds each and all the outside stock, corn and hay. The bed linen, brass, pewter, household goods and implements were to be divided equally among his children. Joseph obviously baulked at the task himself, unlike the family patriarch Thomas who had divided up his chattels so meticulously a hundred and twenty years before. I wonder if this comfortable group of his descendants looked sideways at their Saggers cousins and reflected that the piece of land Joseph was leaving Daniel should have belonged to Mary, who had died the year before her nephew Joseph made his will, aged ninety. The difficulties of her runaway marriage hadn't brought her to an early grave so she may have made the right choice after all.

Thomas 'wheeler' was also making his will with two of the same provisions in it as Joseph's: 'to my loving wife so long as she remains a widow' and an annual sum of money to be paid to one of his sons. Perhaps this was thought the fair thing to do for a youngest son for whom there was no more land to inherit. This descendant of bewitched James left his son James an identifiable piece of the earlier James property called Soules. Son Thomas, also a wheelwright, was to have the house, seventeen acres and five roods, this latter a piece of Stonywork common that had belonged to the earlier James together with two pieces in Middlefield common. Three daughters received between five and fifteen pounds, the married girl getting the least since she had presumably already had a dowry. This Thomas wasn't buried in the parish church either and it's fairly safe to assume that he was another Nonconformist Whig.

In the century of warfare almost unbroken except for the Walpole period that had now begun, the Tory voters Robert and Thomas must have been for peace. This Thomas was probably Robert's brother who had inherited Armigers, which was often known simply as 'the farm'. Their uncle Thomas cordwainer had at last inherited a property, a tenement and parcel of land which John Bernard had left between four people with his own surname and Mary and Thomas Jarvis. John Bernard's wife was buried in the Quaker burial ground at Monk Street, which suggests that Thomas cordwainer was the Quaker in the family and perhaps disliked for that reason. He must have died soon after 1728, when his last payment of rent is recorded.

The church had provided itself with powder and shot in 1690

against a Jacobite invasion, and troops were quartered in Essex in 1697 on their return from William III's Flanders campaign. The bells were rung for victory over the French and the then churchwarden made a trip to Bardfield in 1712 'about taking up of soldiers'. He also gave money that year to disabled soldiers. In the 1730s there were candles provided 'for ye soldiers'.

Thomas Jarvis of Armigers died in 1724. He seems to have been childless for the farm passed out of the family to a John Westwood and his widow Mary sold his other property to Thomas Drane. Thomas had sold some of his land to Thomas wheeler the elder, who passed it on to his son, who was one of the two Jarvis voters in the 1734 election, as a Whig plumper using only one of his votes for Viscount Castlemain.

Robert his brother and his wife Ann Wren, daughter of Will Wren, yeoman, who had left her six acres of land, had had at least nine children. Twice they had named a baby son Robert only to have him die within the year. Their daughters included Dorothy and Millicent, exotic among the Marys and Anns which were still the most popular. Their only surviving son was Thomas. Martha, their fourth daughter, married Thomas Claydon in 1732. Her younger sister Dorothy married William Bentley of Stebbing in 1731. Perhaps it was the strain of finding six dowries that had caused her father that same year to sell what had become known as the Overshot Millhouse and his lands to John Smith, at the same time as an Andrew Jarvis sold his two acres of pasture to an absentee landlord, Thomas Milbourne.

By this sale Robert disenfranchised both himself and his son Thomas who was now sixteen. Robert had therefore no vote in the 1734 election and died the following year at what for a Jarvis was the early age of fifty-seven. Ann outlived him by five years. Unless son Thomas had some trade he would have been forced to become a labourer. All the signs suggest that this was what he did. What had gone wrong?

Robert's wasn't an isolated case that could be put down simply to his mismanagement or ill-health. Of the eighty-three people who voted in the 1734 election thirty-seven family names were missing from the poll of 1768, and only one of them is recorded as belonging to someone too old to make the journey to Chelmsford. The overall number had also dropped to seventy-six or by about eight per cent. Some of the number had been made up from old Thaxted families who had bought up freeholds. Others were newcomers.

Rents, rates and prices were beginning to rise all over the country as a result of the wars and changing conditions which made it increasingly hard for a small farmer to compete. The Dunmow area also had a poor soil which needed enriching by expensive draining and manuring that could only be undertaken by those with capital. The change from pasture to arable after the Elizabethan wool boom was over must have tended too towards an eventual exhaustion of the soil. At the same time the textile industry was declining in Essex, with subsequent loss of jobs and increasing poor rates.

Thaxted is usually said to have been itself a partly textile town but among the roughly 650 wills of Thaxted citizens there are very few indeed of weavers and those are mainly in a group of related families: Bayford, Catlin and Bowtell, plus the isolated cases of George Savidge, Thomas Gray and Edward George. There were some weavers at nearby Stebbing, where Daniel Jarvis weaver had gone, but there don't seem to me to have been enough in the area for their gradual decline to have made such an appreciable difference, except in the home employment of women as spinners, unless Thaxted men did part-time weaving at home and sold the pieces to clothiers in Colchester.

The yeoman farmer with insufficient capital and low acreage was finding survival increasingly difficult as the industrialization of agriculture, inherent in enclosure and the movement towards larger farms, increased. The potential market provided by the growth of London could really only be exploited by those able to grow grain in quantity and transport it. Labour costs were rising and, although the wages weren't enough to cover the price explosion later in the century, they were still more than a small farmer could manage, particularly when combined with an increased poor rate, which was noticeably steeper in the Dunmow area between 1720 and 1740, when Robert Jarvis gave up the struggle. Over the county as a whole poor relief is estimated to have more than doubled between 1735 and 1776.

Some of the cost went on necessary improvements. In 1715 Thomas Jarvis was involved as an overseer of the poor in leasing a house at Bardfield End as a pest house to isolate victims of smallpox and other infectious and lethal diseases. The spread of inoculation as the century progressed helped to reduce the numbers who died from smallpox but it wasn't cheap and was a much lengthier and more disabling operation than today's quick jab.

William Gilder, by contrast with Robert Jarvis, was managing to make a good living, presumably because his father Henry, who died in 1732, had made enough from the Saracen's Head to buy him a fair-sized property. His brother Robert married a girl in Thaxted, Margaret Cole, also in 1732, and two years later his brother Henry signed the settlement certificate allowing him to move from Great Dunmow to Thaxted with his wife and family. You could only move if the parish from which you came would 'own and acknowledge' their responsibility for you so that you could be sent back from your new parish if you became a financial burden on their poor relief. By 1740 the Robert Gilders were living in a cottage in Stoney Lane belonging to Joseph Hall, tanner. Their only recorded child, Robert, had been born and died in Thaxted the year after their marriage.

William and his wife Elizabeth had had six more children after their move to Thaxted, one of whom, Prudence, was 'an infant dying as soon as born'. Their second son, Henry, was described as yeoman at his marriage to Mary Edwards and what should be the eldest, William, was a yeoman freeholder in a list of 1759, aged 'twenty-five'. Something is clearly wrong here. William junior was actually forty-five. There's no evidence of his marriage or having a son himself called William who could by now be twenty-five. Nor is there any entry for the death of a suitable William but that may simply mean that his part of the family was, unlike Henry and James, non-conforming. There's also no mention of him or his children in his father's will which very much suggests that he had died or moved right away.

The Thaxted Gilders were non-voters. Perhaps they felt it was enough that their Great Dunmow cousins voted for the whole family. William's brother Henry died in 1744 leaving his 'beloved wife Frances' a total of nineteen pounds a year and the Saracen's Head with 'all outhouses, stables, barns, gardens etc.', a parcel of copyhold land to his son Henry, and another freehold with gardens and orchards to his daughter Elizabeth now the wife of Samuel Pilbrow. The couple were already living there and it must have formed part of her dowry. Pilbrow was a carpenter.

Young Henry had married a girl called Elizabeth and was living in a house with six acres of land which had once belonged to a surgeon. By Elizabeth who died in childbirth in 1737 he had a daughter Mary and by his second wife Sarah a son Henry. He was unlucky with his wives for she too died in 1749, to be followed by her husband not three months later. The children were left to the care of Samuel Pilbrow and Richard Wyatt, William Gilder's brother-in-law, until they came of age. The Saracen's Head was to be let meanwhile at the 'best rent possible'. No doubt the insurance with the Sun Fire Company of London which his father had so prudently taken out and provided for in his will was to be kept up. His sister Elizabeth Pilbrow had died two years before, after bearing half a dozen children at least three of whom had died too.

The estate was charged with £300 to be paid to Mary at the age of twenty-one, and the interest of £4. 10s per annum per hundred pounds until then was to be 'employed for her education and maintenance', the first mention of education in any of the two families' wills. As his father had done for his wife, Henry made provision for Mary to enter the Saracen's Head and enjoy the rents and profits up to the amount she was entitled to under the will if her payments fell behind. Mary was thirteen when her father died; the young Henry only twelve. She was still unmarried when he too died aged only twenty-eight, leaving a wife Ann but no children and £5 to his sister to buy herself mourning.

Ann Gilder was a rich young widow and Henry, in leaving everything to his 'beloved wife', had laid no embargo on her remarriage. She soon married a young widower of twenty-six, Lionel Luckin, gent.

The Saracen's Head had not been lucky for the Gilders. Perhaps they had fallen into the habit common among publicans of sampling the wares too often. In contrast, yeoman William in Thaxted lived to seventy-nine, gardener Thomas in Widen to seventy, leaving 'all my stock growing and being in the orchards . . . with all the working tools as now belongs to me in the gardening manner' to his son Henry after his wife Jane's death. She was to set up two gravestones, one at his head and one at his feet as if he was afraid he mightn't stay there. The revenant was a familiar figure in songs and old wives' tales.

I must be going, no longer staying,
The burning Thames I have to cross.
Oh I must be guided without any stumble
Into the arms of my dear lass.

'O Willie dear, O dearest Willie,
Where is that colour you'd some time ago?'
'O Mary dear, the clay has changed me
I'm but the ghost of your Willie O.'

The murdered were the most likely to walk, including the bastard children of the Cruel Mother, but any soul might be unquiet, particularly if the living mourned beyond a fit time and wouldn't let it sleep.

Such songs and stories had an important psychological function and weren't merely entertainment. The punishment foretold by her ghostly children for their 'cruel', murdering mother was meant as a deterrent to girls who might do away with their illegitimate children when the temptation was very strong. As it was, the mortality rate for bastards was high. Often there was no need for killing: a touch of neglect, not even conscious but the by-product of shame and misery, was enough when infants were so vulnerable anyway.

In 1749 Joseph the son of Ann Gilder was baptised and buried. Ann was William's daughter, now aged twenty-five. The child's father was young Joseph Bowtell aged nineteen. William leased ten acres of pasture called Stony Fields in Waterlane from Joseph Bowtell senior, who was a gardener. Perhaps this was how the couple met. There's no way of knowing whether they were in love or whether one of them simply seduced the other. My money is rather on Ann in that case, as the elder.

Unlike many such stories this one had an ending we must presume was happy. The year after their baby's birth and death Joseph and Ann were married. The time lapse can be accounted for only by the unwillingness of at least one of the parties involved. Perhaps Joseph wanted to marry her but his father refused his consent. William meanwhile would have been urging the affair on as father of the 'wronged girl'.

The Bowtells were a numerous and many-branched family which had been in Thaxted for as long as the Jarvisses. It included a master of Thaxted grammar school, John, who had sent two of his sons to Cambridge. Joseph senior was buried in the church itself which was always something of an honour. He died in 1768 and his will reveals that young Joseph was merely following in father's footsteps for there are bequests to two illegitimate daughters as well as to his legal family including his son.

Ann too wasn't forgotten in her father's will for he left her fifty pounds. Her brother John was left twenty, Henry a hundred and her sister Elizabeth, now married to Henry Franklin, fifty as well. Thomas, another brother, was already dead but his children Thomas and Elizabeth were left ten pounds each at twenty-one. James, the youngest, was to have the house and lands at Millhill Farm on condition that his mother should have 'the parlour and chamber for her own use. She can lop the trees for dead wood for firing'. She was also to have fifteen pounds a year for life and furniture for her rooms to the value of ten pounds. William's younger brother Robert was to have the sum of two shillings weekly, suggesting a very dependent status in his old age, but both he and his wife died before William, who was quickly followed by Elizabeth 'my beloved wife', as if she had simply pined away.

James's own wife Mary had died the same year and a year later the knell was rung for Henry and the following year for James himself. Mary had also been a member of the Bowtell family, so whatever differences there had been over Ann's base born child between the two families must have been composed before she and James married. Henry's wife, who didn't die until the next century at the age of eighty-five, was the daughter of Solomon Edwards, a miller. Five years after she had married Henry in the presence of her father, her sister Elizabeth married William Jarvis, husbandman, relating the two families by marriage for the first time, though it's hard to fit this William precisely into place, since he wasn't baptised in the parish church although his own children were to be. As I have suggested earlier, he may be a son of Isaac.

Unless Henry Gilder had been married before he married late in life two years short of forty. Mary Edwards was twenty-three and they had nine children before he died at fifty-five. James managed three before he died at only thirty-five. The second generation of Gilders hadn't the longevity of their fathers. James's death made his children orphans with the eldest only eight. It seems very likely that Henry's widow took them in and brought them up with her own brood, the eldest of whom, Elizabeth, was now fifteen and able to help her mother. If so it must have drawn them all together in that closeness that persisted for the next hundred years as they ran in and out of each other's cottages at Cutlers Green, and which still took Maud and the other children back to Granny's for their holidays four generations later.

IN LOVING MEMORY
OF
LYDIA JARVIS
WHO DIED
FEBRUARY
AGED 73 YEARS

PEACE PERFECT PEACE

ALSO OF
SAMUEL JARVIS
WHO PASSED AWAY
JUNE 8TH 1935
AGED 84 YEARS

RE-UNITED

VII   *The Bonny Labourers*

When Morant published his great *History of Essex* in 1768 he was still able to list two Jarvisses among the twenty-seven people having lands in Thaxted. These were Thomas Jarvis wheelwright, now of course the son of the first so described, and Joseph Jarvis 'malster', who owned Totmans where he ran a brewery. Joseph Bowtell is also in the list but there's no mention of William Gilder, which must mean that Morant had some principle of selection that looks as if it was either acreage or local status.

A survey of the manor of Thaxted done in 1770, the year William died and when his lands had just passed to his youngest son James, shows that he had a farm and thirty-five acres. Joseph Jarvis had twenty-four acres and Thomas wheelwright had roughly twenty-five. Totmans had been bought by Joseph's father, Thomas son of Joseph, about 1742 when Joseph married Sara Coleman. Mary Saggers' forfeited piece of Great Aversie Common was still in the family, which, with the continuance of Joseph as a family Christian name, makes it easy to identify this branch. Others are harder.

Robert's son Thomas married Grace Marten also in 1742 and both couples began to produce the inevitable brood of children. Thomas and Grace had eight; Joseph and Sara had a mere three: James, Ann, and the first of the daisy chain of Lydias, who died aged only five. I'm inclined to think that Joseph had been married twice and that by his first wife, Elizabeth who had died in 1732, he had sons Joseph and Thomas and a daughter Elizabeth, all mentioned in his will.

One branch of the Jarvis family, headed by another Joseph, had preferred Great Easton as its parish church but now moved into Thaxted itself on the marriage of his son Patient Jarvis and Mary Searl. Patient's strange name was his mother's surname, a

119

very common one in the area. Great Easton was the next parish, to the south of Thaxted, and the old family property at Stanbrook and Monk Street lay equidistant between the two churches. By 1757 Patient and Mary were living in Thaxted where their son John Patient was baptised and they worked some land belonging to a William Grout.

Tragedy struck repeatedly at another Jarvis couple, William husbandman and Elizabeth Edwards, who were also having children in the middle of the century, for two of their children, Hannah aged five and William aged two, died in 1767, to be followed by Joseph aged one in the next year. At least to us it seems a tragedy but to contemporaries it could seem the opposite: 'my parents had the good fate to have but a small family, I being the eldest of 4, two of whom died in their infancy,' John Clare wrote honestly of his own childhood.

The situation became very different, however, when William himself quickly followed his youngest son leaving Elizabeth a young widow with two little girls, Sarah seven and Elizabeth only four. As a widow she was entitled to the help of the parish and the various charities, and to an almshouse in her old age. In theory no blame attached to her for her dependent state, though her children might grow up on the parish and be apprenticed or sent into service. But perhaps Elizabeth didn't need help. Her father had voted for the two Whig candidates in the 1768 election, along with all the rest of the Thaxted freeholders, except three who voted two for the Tory candidates and one ambiguously for one of either party. Elizabeth's brother-in-law Henry Gilder, yeoman, was also still alive and it may be that she was able to turn to her sister Mary for some support though Mary was soon to have problems enough of her own, left as she was three years later with eight children, the youngest of whom, Thomas, was only one.

1771 was a sickly year in Thaxted though the register offers no explanation for it. Instead of the usual thirty odd burials, there were fifty-eight in the parish church and graveyard, including Mary and Elizabeth's parents within a few weeks of each other, Mary's husband and Grace, the wife of Thomas Jarvis. Both Henry Gilder and Solomon Edwards could have been expected to leave wills but neither of them did, so perhaps whatever epidemic it was struck very suddenly.

Mary must have been the first of the Gilder matriarchs although not herself a born Gilder. Lydia's youngest son still remembers his mother's strength and control over the family. In those words of the deepest approbation for a woman of my childhood, she was 'a good manager' and this tradition could have come down from Mary herself, passed on from mother to daughter, daughter-in-law and niece as she oversaw succeeding generations. She had now become for official purposes Widow Gilder although only just forty.

For a few years there had been peace but a peace that brought not plenty but dearth, famine, unemployment and riot. Essex seems to have escaped the worst of the rioting at the beginning of the previous war with France and again after it, but in 1772 hardship was so great that on April 12, a Sunday: 'About 11 o'clock at night a mob assembled at Chellmsford armed with bludgeons and next day went in a body to visit the mills in that neighbourhood from whence they took great quantities of wheat and wheat flour. At Witham and Sudbury upon the same road they stopt the cars laden with meat for the London markets and exposed it for sale at 3d the pound; the wheat they seize they sell at 4s a bushell and gave the money to the owners.'

This account in *The Gentleman's Magazine* suggests a high degree of organisation and self-restraint at the beginning of the outbreak. In Colchester, where they had had no market the previous Saturday and no meat, corn, meal or flour brought into the town for a week, the butchers were afraid to kill any beasts lest they should be seized by the mob. At Bury a riotous band patrolled the streets by day and night obliging the mealmen and shopkeepers to sell them their commodities at their own prices. Troops were called for, and sent, though the Secretary at War, Lord Barrington, wrote that 'one quarter of a troop is more than enough to make a thousand Essex rioters run away'.

By April 15 the Reverend Mr Tindal, a humane man, had persuaded the people to desist from 'unwarrantable proceedings' and to return home until a subscription could be raised for their relief since provisions were so dear. But his efforts went unappreciated by the Lord Lieutenant, Lord Rochford, who was surprised at talk of a subscription: 'When the distress becomes real, humanity will dictate it; but magistrates if they give way to such an idea, do not surely reflect on the encouragement it must give to idle ill-disposed people.' He promised a troop of dragoons and exhorted the magistrates to make early examples of ringleaders.

This was easier called for than done. It was often some time after the event before men could be identified and arrested. Many of them managed to melt away to London and hide, for the penalties were often severe: hanging or transportation. *The Gentleman's Magazine* commented: 'Letters from every part of the kingdom bring melancholy accounts of the distresses of the poor, and of their readiness to do mischief . . .' But such mischief would only bring worse upon themselves and they were exhorted instead to pray for a good harvest.

One little episode concerning the Jarvis family in this year may be connected with the riots although it's impossible to be certain since a document which might have explained it further has been missing for some years. Andrew Jarvis of Little Saling, yeoman, was summoned for assaulting the bound bailiff Thomas Johnson and enabling his prisoner, Francis Willett junior, to escape.

> Who fattens best where sorrow worst appears
> And feeds on sad misfortune's bitterest tears?
> Such is Bumtagg the bailiff to a hair
> The worshipper and demon of despair . . .

Andrew was a descendant of Daniel via Thomas of Duck End. It was probably his father Andrew of Bardfield Saling who was buried in Lindsell the year after the riots, aged ninety-two. The custom of rescuing an arrested man was an old one and had been practised against an earlier Thomas Jarvis, constable of Thaxted. A gang of the arrested man's friends and relatives would set upon the gaoler and let his victim escape. It may be that Willett junior had committed some more ordinary offence but it may also be that it was political rather than criminal since such unrest was in the air.

Times were hard again six years after the Essex food riots, so hard that in the winter of 1778 the Thaxted churchwardens, following a resolution by the vestry, sold coal and flour at cheap rates to those in want. Flour was sixpence a peck cheaper than 'the common price'. Throughout January, February and March 'James Gilder's children' received eight bushels of coal and three half-pecks of flour, Mary, 'Widow Gilder', had six half-pecks of flour and six pecks of coal, her sister 'Widow William Jarvis' had two half-pecks of flour, her brother-in-law John Gilder had two half-pecks, a Thomas Jarvis one, a Thomas Jarvis of Richmonds Green two and Patient Jarvis, who like Mary Gilder had a flock of children to feed, qualified for five and three bushels of coal.

Clare knew first hand the misery of the rural poor at this time of year:

O winter, what a deadly foe
Art thou unto the mean and low!
What thousands now half pin'd and bare
Are forced to stand thy piercing air
All day, near numbed to death wi' cold
Some petty gentry to uphold,
Paltry proudlings hard as thee,
Dead to all humanity.

I don't know whether the separate entry for James Gilder's children means that they were living by themselves now or whether it merely made accounting easier if the allotments were recorded strictly by family. However, it may be that the three children were living alone. Mary was now fourteen, Elizabeth a year younger and James about eleven. But James was a precocious lad, so much so that he seems to have married two years later, at least there is no one else who could be the James labourer of Thaxted who married Sara Perry in the parish church of Lindsell and whose first child was born in the next year. He would of course have had to go out to work very early, as soon indeed as he could find anyone to take him, and he had no parents to refuse their permission to marry. Even so, he can't have been more than fourteen and may even have had to lie about his age. That may be why the wedding was in another parish.

Thomas Jarvis of Richmond's Green is probably a descendant of Joseph whose daughter married Thomas Saggers and therefore a cousin of the Joseph who was a brewer at Totmans. He held a tenement and about four acres in 1721, paying 2s . 6¾d rent. By 1742 it had passed to a Joseph who must be his son and then vanishes from the records. The Thomas who was able to buy cheaper flour would be Joseph's son become a labourer with the loss of the smallholding. The other Thomas Jarvis should be

Robert's eldest son Thomas, now married and with three children of his own.

The richest of the Jarvisses, Joseph 'malster', died in 1774 leaving his property to his sons Joseph, James and Thomas. James got Totmans and all the cattle and corn about it. Joseph got forty pounds due to his father as executor of the will of his brother Thomas, who had moved to Cambridge and had died there childless. Son Thomas got the lands his father had inherited from brother Thomas in West Wratting. James was to pay annuities of £5 to his mother Sarah, who was also left half a cottage which had been divided in two, of £3 to his sister Ann and to his aunt by marriage, whose husband had bequeathed the Cambridge properties, £10. A married daughter Elizabeth got twenty pounds. When James, who had married Ann Pettit in 1770, died childless in 1786 leaving her all his freehold at Totmans with barns and malthouse, it was to be the last Jarvis will for a century and a half. Henceforth they would have nothing to warrant the effort and expense of a will. Maud when she was grown up would say succinctly: 'They had nothing to leave.'

Thomas Jarvis 'wheeler' died too in the seventies, leaving no will and no record of his burial, only an entry in the manor court records of 1779 that notes the passing of the last of bewitched James's lands to Thomas's nieces Sarah Hurell, Mary Crely and Ann Legge, 'whereupon there happened to the Lord for a fine fifteen shillings according to the custom of this manor'.

About 1761 two Robert Jarvisses were born, neither of whom appears in the Thaxted register. Suddenly, because of the popularity of Clive of India, Robert was as common as Thomas. They could have been the son of Patient and Mary, and the son of Thomas and Grace who had already named one boy Robert after Thomas's father eighteen years before. Certainly two Roberts were buried with ages that would make them born about this year. Such fashions confuse family trees. One of them may be explained by an entry at Great Easton of a Robert, illegitimate son of Sarah in 1762. Sarah may be any of two or three girls so named, perhaps the daughter of John and Mary of Chickney and sister of Martha who had three 'baseborn' children over the course of eight years by a man who is called in the registers Richard Traveller, which I suspect means that he was a gipsy.

As each labourer Jarvis moved out into one of the surrounding villages in search of work on the bigger farms, so he began a branch of the family there until there was none without its new shoot from Thomas Jarvis's old stock. Clare records how the links were kept: 'Children and kin from neighbouring towns around' came to the yearly village feast and at Christmas there was

The welcome sight of little toys
The Christmas gift of cousins round.

Sometimes, as in the case of Patient Jarvis, some of their sons would be forced out of the new place back to Thaxted itself to begin the cycle again.

Servants, women and men, including labourers, were hired for the year at an annual statute fair, except for those employed seasonally for special jobs like ploughing, hoeing and harvesting. The wages in the Thaxted area were twenty pence a week and beer in winter and two shillings in summer. At harvest it was four shillings and tuppence a week with six or seven pints of ale, and for reaping from six and six to as much as twelve shillings a week. Prices of staple foods rose alarmingly from 1767 to 1805. Butter went up to thirteen pence a pound, cheese to eightpence and all meats by over seventy per cent. A labourer's weekly wage in winter would have bought him a pound of butter and a pound of cheese. No wonder that the vicar of Great Dunmow, John Howlett, who took a great interest in local economics and, as well as publishing books of his own, was a correspondent of the Board of Agriculture, argued that 'no contrivance short of adaptation of wages to the price of provisions' would bring down the poor rates or make the poor as well fed and clothed as they had been sixty years before.

The hiring or statute fair, which seems to us now more like a human cattle market, and where indeed the men and women appeared to Clare to go 'like hogs to Lunnon mart', was the ideal place for the recruiting sergeant too. The attractions of the soldiers with their ready money and bright uniforms charmed both boys and girls. The girls would leave their regular boy friends and go off round the fair with a soldier, only to find their sweethearts drunk and dressed in uniform when they got back.

As they would pull and scold great tumults rose;

The sergeant's honour totter'd terribly,
From women's threat'nings hardly 'scap'd with blows;
They'd box his cap about his ears, if he
Gave not the contest up and set the prisoner free.

There were the ballad singers with their printed sheets for those who could read, who would teach the words to the rest. Unlike his father William, Henry Gilder made his mark and both his and James's children were illiterate. After a brief excursion into letters both families had slipped back into that intellectual darkness, 'the shroud of ignorance' that limited conversation

To nothing more than labour's rude employs
'Bout work being slack, and rise and fall of bread,
And who were like to die and who were like to wed.

Yet there were compensations. Many people knew at least a hundred songs by heart and sang them both on their way to and from work and to enliven the sameness of repeated jobs, and there was as much story-telling of folk and fairy-tale coupled with local history as among the Grimms' Black Forest peasants, by mothers and grandmothers at the end of the working day, while the children sat on the sanded cottage floor that Lydia's youngest son still remembers from his visits to Cutlers Green.

While the women talked they span, though they could earn only about fourpence a day from this by 1790 in the Dunmow area where in 1750 they had earned eightpence. They could also sometimes earn about eightpence a day for a short time at such jobs as hand-hoeing wheat, or helping to dibble in young plants including the potato, 'this root to which in modern times an importance has been attached which fifty years ago was unthought of', as the secretary of the Board of Agriculture Arthur Young wrote in 1805, adding that it was 'more largely cultivated in Essex than perhaps in any other southern county'.

But there was little of it grown around Thaxted. The soil was known locally as 'poor red land': 'a weak, thin skinned poor wet loam of loose texture; when dry of a light brown colour, upon a cold stiff whitish clay, as it is called, but really a clay marl, produces nothing without draining; and is a poor soil when improved.' What was now an old-fashioned four-yearly crop rotation, fallow, wheat, fallow, barley, was strictly followed on the poorest Thaxted land, while on the slightly better a year of clover, peas or beans replaced one of the fallows. 'In thirteen miles I saw three scraps of turnips and three or four small fields of cole,' Young reported in disgust.

The yields even with this system were low by comparison with other areas in the county. At twenty-two bushels per acre Thaxted, Lindsell and Great Easton were a low average for wheat while for barley at twenty-six Thaxted was poor indeed compared with the best yields of forty or even forty-eight in a few places. It was this poor return, coupled with enclosure, that had destroyed so many small farmers, not that enclosure needed to be forcibly practised on any great scale in this area. As tenants gave up the struggle their land could be added to the larger farms, which then contributed further to the downfall of the remaining smallholders.

Howlett wrote: 'The small farmer is forced to be laborious to an extreme degree; he works harder and fares harder than the common labourer; and yet with all his labour, and with all his fatiguing incessant exertions, seldom can he at all improve his condition, or even with any degree of regularity pay his rent and preserve his present situation. He is confined to perpetual drudgery which is the source of profound ignorance . . . The little farmer, his family and cattle half-starved, himself worn to the bones with unavailing labour, and perpetual anxiety, can at length pay neither rent, nor rates, nor tithes.'

Once taken over the land could be improved, and Howlett thought well of the new breed of opulent farmers. But Clare lamented the passing of . . . the old freedom that was living then,

When masters made them merry with their men,
When all their coats alike were russet brown,
And his rude speech was vulgar as their own.

The class divisions sharpened as the ranks of the labourers were swelled by dispossessed yeomen and their children which kept wages down with the bigger labour pool and the improved techniques that needed fewer hands.

There were not many improvements in management in the Thaxted area however, in spite of the inventive Mr Knight, who had patented a new mole plough for draining, that needed fifteen horses, three abreast, and six or eight men or boys, and could lay drains through ten acres in eight hours with a saving of seven hundred per cent. This apart, Arthur Young found the farmers 'as torpid as their rotation. If they had more objects in their husbandry they would think more; but they are asleep, and awake only to silent contempt at any propositions of change'.

Rents were low but Young thought that such unimaginative farming didn't deserve to raise them. 'If they examine the tables of the prices of wheat and barley (the only products of the district), they will find that those prices do not permit a rise: it is not very wise to adhere to products, the prices of which have nearly stood still (scarcities excluded), instead of introducing others.' Young suggested that they did so little that they would have been better off sitting in the chimney corner while compound interest on their savings produced the same profit.

There were few cows in the district, which meant that even skim milk, which the poor might buy in other areas, wasn't available there. There was also a painful shortage of fuel as lands were bought up, woods grubbed and commons cleared and 'curst improvement 'gan his fields enclose'. The poor responded in desperation by tearing down hedges and pollarding every tree they could reach for firewood. No wonder William Gilder had been at such pains to ensure his wife's firing in his will. The Thaxted churchwardens in making coal available at a cheaper rate probably had an eye to preventing hedge breaking, since the office was still filled by the local lesser gentry though the numbers of those available for such posts decreased as yeomen became labourers.

To Clare:
> Inclosure came, and every path was stopt;
> Each tyrant fixed his sign where paths were found,
> To hint a trespass now who crossed the ground:
> Justice is made to speak as they command . . .
> . . . And every village owns its tyrants now,
> And parish-slaves must live as parish Kings allow.

Young noted from an earlier survey two hundred acres of waste forest land in the Dunmow district, which by enclosure he reckoned could bring the proprietor an annual improvement of fifteen shillings an acre, and a hundred and forty acres of common that would bring an extra 11s 6d. 'So much has been said on the subject of enclosing . . . and their beneficial tendency towards the improvement of agriculture and the increase of population, salubrity etc so clearly and satisfactorily proved, that it is quite unnecessary to add anything further,' the Reverend Mr. Howlett remarked. But Young clearly felt this wasn't enough for he included in his book on Essex agriculture a panegyric on enclosure suggesting that it was the true basis of patriotism for such were the benefits that 'the peasant who derives his support from the produce of the earth and his own industry, would lay down his life in its defence and support'.

Industry began in summer at six in the morning and went on until six at night. For part of winter it began at seven and stopped at five and for the rest was quite simply dawn till dusk. Sometimes it was piecework and in the long summer days a labourer 'if vigorous, active and industrious' might work from four in the morning until eight at night but such efforts wore down 'the very strongest constitution very fast' and brought on old age 'long before its usual period'.

Harvest was the peak time for work. In many cases the labourers were boarded at the farm for a month to six weeks while their children and wives came out to glean in the cut fields. But even this was changing. The more opulent farmers or rather their wives no longer wanted 'the fatigue and trouble' of boarding, particularly as it now meant maintaining two households in one, for the farmer's family no longer ate with the men at the oak table in the hall

Where master, son and serving man and clown
Without distinction daily sat them down,
Where the bright rows of pewter by the wall
Served all the pomp of kitchen or of hall . . .

Clare was particularly contemptuous of the new farmers' daughters, 'the Ladies of the Farm', who learned at school to scorn 'to toil or foul their fingers more'. Disappointed love might be thought to have over-sharpened his tone except that the folksong shares the note.

No wonder that butter's a shilling a pound,
See those rich farmers' daughters how they ride up and down.
If you ask them the reason they say, 'Bon alas.

There is a French war and the cows have no grass.'
Singing:
Honesty's all out of fashion,
These are the rigs of the time.

Young, quoting Howlett, remarked on the more genteel and respectable appearance of the richer farmers, the sending of their sons and daughters to boarding school and the replacement of good strong beer by red port.

The class differences were heightened by dress. The labourer wore a smock and broad hat for work; his wife by a change of apron showed that she had moved from work to leisure. Lydia's youngest son remembers his Gilder grandmother putting on her clean apron before she sat down to tea in the almshouse she lived in as of right as a widow. By my childhood this had come down to taking off the apron before tea or the arrival of a visitor. 'I was caught with my apron on,' Maud will still say to explain the unexpectedness of a visitor.

But, poor and patched as their clothes were and subtly differing in kind from those of the masters and their ladies, labourers, men and women, still had their best to bring out for the feast in July 'when villagers put on their bran new clothes'

And milk maids drest like any ladies gay
Threw 'cotton drabs' and 'worsted hose' away.

Clare speaks of the girls' sun-tanned faces and their attempts to whiten them with fumitory. The fashions of the farmers' daughters had their effect on the labourers' girls. Now that the ladies were no longer 'as red and rosy as the lovely Spring' but 'pale and bedrid', the maids too tried 'to scare the tan from summer's cheek'. About this time there begins to appear in the Thaxted burial registers the phrase 'of a consumption', showing that pallor didn't always have to be artificially induced. In 1781 two of Mary Gilder's daughters died: Sara, just twenty-one, was buried on November 11 and Charlotte only thirteen on Christmas Day. The death rate this year was very high again at fifty. Poor diet and the overcrowded cottages, many still of wattle and daub, without running water or proper lavatories, were a propagating ground for tuberculosis. Most likely Sara and Charlotte had shared the same bed.

Two years later there began to appear in the registers, following an Act of Parliament, the designation 'pauper' beside many names. A tax was now payable for burials and baptisms and only the indigent were exempt. The first Jarvis to be so labelled was William, born and died in 1785, the son of Sara; 'she on enquiry was unlawfully married to Will Gardner as he had a wife alive.'

Soldier soldier won't you marry me
With your musket, fife and drum?
Oh no sweet maid I cannot marry thee
For I've got a wife of my own.

The unfortunate Sara seems to have been the daughter of the equally unlucky Elizabeth, Mary Gilder's sister, otherwise Widow William Jarvis. It may be that it was her other daughter Elizabeth who produced baseborn Ruth Everitt Jarvis four years later, though for her mother's sake I rather hope it was Elizabeth, daughter of Patient Jarvis. Ruth was a common name for illegitimate girls who could thus be easily suspected as such for the rest of their lives. Everitt was presumably her father's name. It was an old one in the town and two of them had voted in the 1768 election. Strangely, a Thomas Everitt, widower, who was literate enough to sign the register, married Sara Jarvis only three years after the birth of Ruth, who, as usual, vanishes. It could be a plot worthy of Greek tragedy if Thomas had married the sister of the girl he got pregnant, as soon as his wife was dead.

Come now, my love, and sit down by me,
Beneath this green lofty oak where the leaves are springing
    green,
It's now very near three quarters of a year,
Since you and I together have been.

I will not come and sit down beside you,
Nor no other young man;
Since you have been courting some other young girl,
Your heart is no longer mine.

The early eighties were full of trouble for Mary Gilder whether it was her own daughter Elizabeth now aged thirty-three and 'should have known better' or James's, seventeen, 'young and silly', who gave birth to the charmingly named Molly, who suffered the only too common infant death of bastards in the year after Mary's other two girls died. Baseborn female children rarely, unlike Ruth Jarvis, give any clue to their fathers. Molly is a slightly unusual name for this time when Moll still had the meaning of whore and Molly was more often used for a homosexual man. Perhaps it implies that her father was an Irishman. Five years later William and Sarah Jarvis also came up with an unusual name for their daughter when they combined their own and called her simply Sall.

Mary must have been glad to get two of the Gilder girls married in the next few years and both not to labourers: Mary married a carpenter and Ann a journeyman butcher, two useful tradesmen to add to the family. Then it was her son William's turn. He was twenty-eight and a member of the Independent Church and he married, in the parish church by licence as non-conformists often did, Rebecca Byatt. It was William who began the religious tradition which Samuel Jarvis took over when he married Lydia Gilder, so that their son could say of them, 'They were chapel people.' Perhaps William hadn't become one until he married Rebecca. Certainly in my childhood it was felt that the wife set the religious tone while the husband saw to the political.

It wasn't only in religion that William was different from the rest of his family. Unlike the other sons of Henry and James he was certainly by 1801, if not before, a farmer not a labourer. It looks very much as if Mary his mother had in some way kept part of his father Henry's estate for him, either as money or land, while still claiming her various widow's benefits. At any rate he leased a farm at Cutlers Green from the trustees of the Dunmow charity and by the beginning of the new century when the poor rate was four shillings in the pound he was assessed at £1 12s.

There are no local Gilders in the 1782 land tax list but plenty of Jarvisses, at least ten of whom are definite descendants of the original Thomas. They had holdings in Bardfield Saling, Great Bardfield, Stebbing, Lindsell and Steeple Bumpstead but in Thaxted itself there was only James the brewer, who died childless before the decade was over. However, what had already overtaken Thaxted spread gradually through the surrounding parishes so that by the time of the 1838 electoral register only the Stambourne/Steeple Bumpstead branch had members qualified to vote, among whom, I'm glad to see, was one Thomas.

The labourer's year began with the November ploughing, that's to say it never ended but was a segment of a continuous cycle into which his own life fitted like an extended year with its seasons, and this bred an acceptance of the unchanging, unchangeableness of things. Winter was the time for threshing, the job most detested by Clare, pent all day in a barn, choked by clouds of dust, dulled by the continued whop, whop of the flail, which was the origin of the soldiers' name for country lads: 'whopstraws'.

Cows still had to be milked and sheep tended, even in deepest winter, but perhaps the most freezing job of all when the leaves were off the branches was the hedger's, in leather coat and mittens 'chopping the pattering bushes hung with dew' or laced with snow, and bringing home a bundle of firewood as his perks at the end of the day. Then came the spring ploughing: three horses, a man and a boy at seven shillings the acre in 1805 in the Dunmow district, which was lower pay than anywhere else in the county.

The ploughmen were the princes of the agricultural labourers as their logical and often literal descendants the railwaymen were to be in town. Ploughboys are always pretty:

A pretty little ploughboy a-driving of his team
  And his horses stood under the shade.
'Tis all for your sweet sake I come this way
  And so I'm rewarded for my pains.

So sings the girl whose pursuit gets him taken by the press gang and sent to the fleet. Essex, according to Arthur Young, abounded 'with skilful and accurate ploughmen'.

Drilling and dibbling were beginning to be practised by the end of the eighteenth century but there was still much broadcast sowing in the biblical style, and farmers watched those foolhardy enough to try new ways with 'no little pleasantry and merriment' when things seemed to be going wrong. Hoeing and weeding took up the spring, jobs that the women could earn a little extra at. By June it was time to begin mowing the hay and bringing in the sheep for washing and clipping, such few sheep as there were round Thaxted. Meanwhile the ploughmen would be summer-ploughing the fallows until they had been turned as many as five times.

Children of course worked too, bird-scaring, minding the cattle and with hay and other harvests. Often a child was alone all day, with perhaps a working dog for company, asking the time eagerly of any stray passerby to see how 'the enemy' was going. It was better toiling together in a group in the meadows, turning and cocking the hay, with the stories of the old grannies to look forward to when they plumped down in the shade at dinner time, flinging up their skirts for coolness and passing round a snuffbox while they yarned and the bottles of small beer were uncorked.

For the grain harvest the whole of a small village might be emptied. Thaxted of course was bigger than this, though the population had fallen in the eighties to 1,769, the vicar noted. It was long, hard, sweaty graft but at the end there was the harvest home feast with every excuse for getting drunk, making love, dancing and singing. Many reformers blamed the alehouse for the state of the poor but Arthur Young, while not condoning drunkenness and no radical, understood the motive for much of it. 'Go to an alehouse kitchen . . . and there you will see the origin of poverty and poor rates. For whom are we to be sober? For whom are we to save? For the parish? If I am diligent shall I have leave to build a cottage? If I am sober, shall I have land for a cow? If I am frugal, shall I have half an acre for potatoes? You offer me no motives, you have nothing but a parish officer and a workhouse. Bring me another pot.'

With the larger farms, people worked further away from each other. The ploughman might be all day going up and down turning the furrows on some distant field with only the horses to sing or whistle to, the hedger might have to trudge miles home at night from his far-off section. This was one effect of enclosure. At the same time a degree of factory farming, as we now call it, was being introduced, in the fattening of stall-tethered animals, which sprang indirectly from the loss of the beast's right, as Clare puts it, to the free acres of the common along with man's.

The sheep and cows were free to range as then
Where change might prompt, nor felt the bonds of men.
Cows went and came with every morn and night

To the wild pasture as their common right;
And sheep, unfolded with the rising sun,
Heard the swains shout and felt their freedom won,
Tracked the red fallow field and heath and plain,
Or sought the brook to drink, and roamed again;
While the glad shepherd traced their tracks along,
Free as the lark and happy as her song.

Both men and animals were enslaved by the changed conditions which we have now exacerbated to the point where
many people are revolted by the methods of much of our
agriculture which, I believe, were hatched in the late eighteenth
century. The sufferings of two- and four-legged animals were
often inextricably interwoven. The conversion of pasture to
arable following enclosure was offset by feeding the new root
crops to livestock kept indoors, with the consequent loss of jobs
to shepherds and cowboys. The term husbandman itself disappears under the all-embracing 'labourer'.

Young James Gilder's first wife Sarah didn't last long. After
bearing three sons, James, Joseph and William, she died in 1793
and was buried as a pauper. James soon remarried. He was only
in his mid-twenties. His new wife was Margaret Mason and she
bore him two sons, John and Thomas. They had married by
licence so it's likely that one of them, like brother William, was
non-conformist, and probably it was James since Margaret was
buried in the parish churchyard, in 1819 aged forty-six, while
there's no sign of the burial of James. He must be presumed
buried in the Independent graveyard unless he died in another
parish away from Thaxted.

The entries of the Independent Church have mostly vanished,
apart from a record of baptisms from 1790 to 1836, and the
parish records themselves are very suspect for this period. In
1781 Henry Maynard, a younger brother of the lord of the
manor in whose gift the living was, became vicar at only twenty-
two, following the contemporary custom of putting one son in
the army and one in the church. He died in 1806, aged only
forty-seven, so perhaps he hadn't been strong enough to care
properly for the parish. At first his curate seems to have kept the
registers up to scratch with very full entries but after 1786 there's
nothing, apart from the ominous and by then monotonous

symbol for a pauper, to identify an entry in the burial register as adult or child, widow or wife. In 1796 the months from March to September were left out altogether and three years later there were only twelve burials recorded for a whole year. It's possible of course that so many people had left Thaxted at that time that the figure is an accurate reflection of the true number, for Britain was at war again and many of the men, desperate for work, had gone for a soldier.

VIII *Paupers and Redcoats*

Whether virtually the whole town had decided it was wiser to be registered as paupers rather than pay the new fees, or whether they were indeed all legitimately exempt is impossible to say. Of the thirty-nine people buried in 1793, only nine weren't designated paupers, while the figures for baptisms are even higher. Only the baptisms of William and Rebecca Gilder's children of all the Jarvis and Gilder entries for the period aren't so marked and that may be more because they were nonconformist than because he was a farmer. What must have been a deeply resented practice stops in 1795. Meanwhile it had included four of the children of Robert and Martha Jarvis, one of whom, Samuel, was the grandfather of Samuel who would marry Lydia Gilder. It seems to us now peculiarly repugnant that a child should be dubbed 'pauper' at its christening.

Much was later to be made of 'the pauperization of the labouring class' which was seen by the theorists as the evil effect of too low wages and too great dependence on various forms of poor relief. The labourer, it was argued, lost his independence when he came to rely on charity, while those who had to pay the high poor rates artificially depressed wages. Much better, it was later said, to pay men more for their work and preserve their dignity. Yet this was an over-simplification when nearly a whole town could be termed 'pauper' by a change in the law.

Besides, it wasn't the higher wages that really brought about a slight improvement in the labourer's lot but a fall in prices because of better harvests and an end to some of the distortions of an economy which constantly fluctuated between war and peace. It needed only a new run of bad harvests, including the now staple potato, to call up the hungry forties. There was to be no true bettering of the poor's condition until 1914. While

nineteenth-century statesmen and commentators were congratu-
lating themselves on having solved the problems of the
eighteenth century by taking the poor off the parish, Flora
Thompson's labourers at 'Lark Rise', though able to eat on ten
shillings a week, found it almost impossible to shoe and clothe
themselves, and had no alternative but the workhouse or moving
in with their children when the man was too old to earn enough
to pay the rent, a situation that was only remedied by the
introduction of the state old age pension. She records how the
first recipients wept as they collected their money at the post
office and brought little presents for the girl clerk whose only
contribution was to hand it to them.

A succession of bad harvests in the 1790s, combined with the
fear that the revolutionary ideas from France might spread among
the British, caused new subscriptions to be raised in Essex to
supply the barley loaf at sixpence, while at the Quarter Sessions
a meeting of millers and magistrates in June 1794 resolved that
only flour with a high percentage of bran should be made and
the judges and grand jury ate only bread made from this during
the assize.

For a time white wheaten bread disappeared from the tables of
both rich and poor, from those of the rich by choice and from the
poor by necessity. Barley bread is an unappetizing colour, a kind
of livid grey, and of a dense puddingy consistency that soon goes
dry to become like a stone. The poor also ate bread that was half
beanflour and no doubt very nutritious, as was that with a high
proportion of bran. But these dark breads were deeply resented
with a strength that persisted into my childhood against all the
exhortations of the nutritionists. Maud still claims that brown
bread is indigestible. The white loaf became a symbol of working-
class aspirations like the white faces of the farmers' wives and
daughters. Consumer goods — and fashions are part of them —
can't be restricted to any one class of British society but as soon as
they appear they are, in theory at least, within the reach of all.
Brown bread became itself a symbol of poverty. In the south,
Arthur Young remarked, bread was still the staple food and he
noted the poor's distaste for anything other than the white loaf,
while a mid-nineteenth-century historian remarked that the 'pure
white loaf' was 'now to be found at the humblest table'.

In December 1795 *The Gentleman's Magazine* reported from

Essex and the surrounding counties in an enquiry into the late dearth: 'The poorer people rejected wheaten bread [with a high bran content] not so much because they thought it unwholesome, or did not like it, but because it was not universal: if there was no other sort they would be content to eat it.'

In fairness to the authorities it has to be allowed that they were at least concerned: there was no 'Let them eat cake', indeed wheaten pastry was forbidden. The King set up a mill in Windsor Great Park to grind flour for the local poor, to be sold to them at 5s 4d per bushel. The Lord Mayor and council forbade the use of hair powder. Many of the nobility issued joint declarations that they would eat only the standard loaf. Yet still the poor rioted in their desperation, the troops were called, the Act was read, those that could be caught were. An Act was passed against seditious meetings which were thought to be nests for French agents.

Thaxted too had its moments of sedition on March 4, 1793, when there seems to have been an attempt by an Isaac Seer, 'otherwise the Royal George', to organize some kind of strike among the labourers. His nickname strongly suggests that he had been a sailor on one of the ships of the line of the same name. He was probably the Isaac Seer who married Susan Legerton from a local yeoman stock, at Great Easton in 1780. The Sears — the name is variously spelt — weren't a strictly Thaxted family but they were undoubtedly local. Isaac was arrested in the evening as a 'disorderly person' at the Sun in Thaxted by William Burton, constable. What happened to him after I've been unable to discover but there's no mention of the episode in either the *Chelmsford Chronicle* or *The Gentleman's Magazine* so it looks as if his attempt was unsuccessful. March seems a bad time of year to pick for an agricultural strike. Such attempts as there were tended to be at harvest time, when the farmers' anxiety to get the crop in before the weather changed and the corn was spoiled could be used as a lever. Isaac seems to have tried the same thing with the spring sowing and perhaps failed because it didn't command the same degree of urgency.

In 1792 Joseph and James Jarvis had married Elizabeth Taylor and Elizabeth Harvey and their first children were also labelled pauper, like the children of Robert and Martha Jarvis. They may have been sons of Patient Jarvis who had been buried as a pauper the year before. The first names and ages would fit but the presence of Clement Grout, who, together with Ann, the widow of James, had inherited the brewery at Totmans, at the wedding of James suggests that he may have been a close relative of James 'malster'. If so, then the collapse of the small farmer and his inability to keep his sons from the route of labourer to pauper is even more marked.

Yet life had to go on. People still fell in love, married and had sex which led to the inevitable children, even though there was little to feed them on. However, there's a gap in the marriages for both families of nearly ten years, until 1803, in the parish records. That year John Roberts widower married one of the Elizabeth Gilder cousins, daughter of either James or Henry, one of whom was forty-three and the other thirty-eight, when the gossips must have said they had missed their chance.

Mother I longs to get married
I longs to be a bride . . .
My maidenhead does grieve me
That fills my heart with fear.
It is a burden, a heavy burden
It's more than I can bear.

The last Jarvis to be buried as an official pauper in this period was the infant son of James and Elizabeth, John, and a John too was the last Gilder to be so described, aged sixty-nine and the only surviving son of William. Once again the irony of the situation is pointed up in that his father had been able to leave him twenty pounds in his will. At the very end of the century, when the pauper entries had been abandoned, two Thomas Jarvisses were buried within two years of each other, the second of whom was Thomas Jarvis of Stanbrook, who had been sufficiently well off to pay the overseers of the poor a pound in poor rate. Perhaps he was the Thomas descendant of Abraham the miller via Robert, while the other was descended from that Thomas whose sister had run away to marry Thomas Saggers. There's nothing in the records to show, any more than there is for the Mary, probably wife of one of them, who died in 1801, but these are the two likeliest.

Meanwhile the rout had begun again with the new threat from France. A revised Militia Act of 1757 now meant that men were chosen by ballot for three months' service at a time and could be sent out of their own county, which had to provide arms for them instead of their parish. If the lot fell on you, you could buy yourself off with a substitute. Such was John Jarvis who served in Captain John Nunn's company at Thaxted in 1781 and 1782. The company had a captain, a lieutenant, an ensign, three sergeants, three corporals, two drummers and fifty-one privates. They marched to Westfield Camp to train there.

By 1795 invasion seemed a real possibility and a complete muster of the county was drawn up. The militia was divided into East and West Essex, which made separate returns. Among the over six hundred privates of the West Essex Militia was Robert Jervice, who served for three years at least, and the unmistakeable surnames of other Jarvis connections, in particular Jealous and Juniper, though unfortunately without a parish for absolute identification.

As the threat of invasion grew stronger Thaxted like many other Essex towns raised its own corps of volunteers, with the son of the schoolmaster-cum-registrar John Frye as drill sergeant, Robert Arnold, Thomas Wooley and John Willett as sergeants, and that most important post of all, without which none of them would have kept in step (nor would the villagers on their march have known when to come out and wave), drummer, filled by Thomas Frye, no doubt the drill sergeant's young brother, and Lasjell Leader, a descendant of the Elizabethan vicar. There were no Jarvisses or Gilders among the sixty privates, who included Joseph Bowtell, Charles Saggers, John Byatt and John Patient as well as Turners and Smiths, all under the command of Captain Richard Maitland. In 1805 the volunteers were at Epping camp, where Maitland signed the accounts on his 'word and honour as an officer and a gentleman'. Unfortunately there was an error in the meat and baggage charge. One of the attractions of the volunteers must have been the three quarters of a pound meat allowance per man per day, at a total cost of £17 8s 6d in a time when the families left behind might only see meat once a week.

The general militia was intended to be a recruiting ground for front line troops and it seems to have been very successful. The men who had formed Elizabeth's militia for defence against Spanish invasion had been mainly yeomen who could supply their own arms. Now it was their descendants who trained against the French but as labourers who even while they trained

143

were the butt of the kind of jokes which would never have been levelled against their forefathers. How either would have fared if put to the test of an invasion is as speculative as the fate of the Home Guard in the Second World War if Hitler had landed.

Meanwhile when the West Essex camped at Freshwater in the Isle of Wight in 1805, they included in Captain W. Boggis's company Thomas Drane and one of the Glascocks, a George Jarvice in Captain R. Boggis's and in Captain Richard Townsend's a Benjamin Jarvice and a Joseph Guilder.

The various Jarvisses may or may not be members of the family but there's no mistaking Joseph Guilder, as the army spelt him. He was the second son of James labourer and Sarah, born in 1783. He had joined the militia at Epping in October 1803, when he was twenty-one. Benjamin Jarvice stayed on at Freshwater with the militia but Joseph volunteered to transfer to the Fifth Northumberland Regiment of Foot who were stationed briefly at Hilsea, Portsmouth. Perhaps he had heard on the barrack grapevine that their next stop would be Colchester and wanted to see Essex, his family and perhaps a girl for the last time before setting out on his new career, which might mean almost continuous service overseas. He took his £1 13s 0d owed him by the West Essex and joined the Fifth in April.

Joseph was twenty-three, with hazel eyes, light brown hair, and a fresh complexion, and five foot four and a half inches tall. It's the nearest I've come to a family portrait until the photograph of Samuel and Lydia, this verbal sketch on his discharge papers. The regiment was on its way back from Guernsey and was being brought up to full strength of a thousand rank and file in the first battalion. The second battalion was stationed at Chichester, having been embodied (curious word) at Horsham the year before. Perhaps the strangest use of the term is in its reverse 'disembodied', as the West Essex were described after the French threat was over and only the officers were kept on the establishment.

Thaxted had had its 'foreign' troops too and perhaps one of them was the father of Molly Gilder baseborn. James Meade, a private in the West Kent Militia, was buried in the church in 1780, two years before Molly's birth and death, and James Sperahier, soldier in 1795. In riotous times it was difficult to call out the local militia against their own starving relatives. The new

Militia Act, by sending them away from home and importing strangers into the district with no ties, helped to control the country. Many of the militia commanders questioned whether it was right to use militia at all, rather than regular troops, for riot duty, but by making the militia the chief recruiting ground for the front line troops the distinction could be easily blurred.

The new war with France was, however, popular enough to distract attention from evils at home, unlike the War of American Independence which was generally disliked in Essex as a species of civil war, with meetings being held against it in Chelmsford and a petition drawn up. Boney was a different matter, feared by small children as a bogeyman who would 'get' them if they weren't good, and respected as an enemy. Even so not everyone was eager for war, certainly not the girls left behind.

> Cruel, cruel was the war when first the rout began
> And out of Old England went many a smart young man
> They pressed my love away from me, likewise my brothers three
> They sent them to the war, my love in the Isle of Germany.
> The drum that my love's beating is covered with green,
> The pretty lambs is sporting, 'tis pleasure to be seen,
> And when my pretty babe is born sits smiling on my knee
> I'll think upon my own true love in the Isle of Germany.

The first battalion the Fifth were reviewed by the Duke of York in Colchester in the autumn and embarked in November for the defence of Hanover. Joseph thus became, as far as I know, the first member of either family to go abroad, unless a Henry Gilder who shipped to Barbados in 1635 is a progenitor. I hope Joseph wasn't in the transport *Helder*, which was wrecked off the Helder and all those on board taken prisoner by the Dutch. They were exchanged after the rest of the battalion had returned to England in the following year, in time to set out on a nine-month voyage to Monte Video, where they took part in the abortive attack on Buenos Aires. The Fifth of course did their bit of the fighting faultlessly but others weren't as successful and the town was abandoned. On the long voyage home there was a shortage of food and water and the men must have been glad to reach Cork.

In his first two years of regular soldiering Joseph had seen

145

Europe and South America, sailed over six thousand miles, marched through swamps and with fixed bayonet under a hail of bullets delivered from the flat roofs of Buenos Aires. He must have liked the life for he stayed with the regiment for just a few months short of twenty years. Joseph enjoyed a spell of rest in Ireland before setting sail to do his bit for the future Duke of Wellington in the Peninsular War, where the regiment became known as 'Wellington's Bodyguard'.

For this campaign Wellington ordered pigtails cut off, heads washed and an issue of sponges for the purpose. Many of the men protested at losing the manly, military queue but their commander had worse in store. The Portuguese were friendly: hats were to be doffed and the Host saluted as it passed in procession through the streets. There was to be no rape. Six camp followers were to be chosen by ballot to every hundred men before embarkation. Their rations would be half those of the soldiers, which were a pound of meat and a pound of biscuit a day and wine when the meat was salt. The women got no wine. The punishment for rape was a brutal flogging or even execution. The girls left behind howled and swooned, but for those who were wives rather than fancy women it was probably best. Joseph had no wife to follow the camp and no doubt slept naked with three other 'hulking fellows', as Wellington called them, in a wooden crib, which the commander constantly tried to replace with hammocks.

The militia provided a better soldier than the old army filled with pressed men and commuted convicts. That steadiness which Wellington so relied on must have derived from the same quality in the rural labourer, together with his physical hardiness from working outdoors in all weathers. It enabled Private Joseph Guilder to endure the terrible retreat that preceded Corunna, when Sir John Moore was killed and a still to this day unknown number of the Fifth. But the life was hard and, unlike the militia, the regulars were unpaid. Looting was therefore commonplace and the women with their babies in their arms were some of the worst offenders. 'The ladies', as Wellington called them, were liable to thirty-six lashes on the bare backside if caught.

And now she is a soldier's wife
And sails across the brine-o.

146

'The drum and fife is my delight
And a merry man in the morning.'

Joseph's battalion returned to England after Corunna and was
then sent on the disastrous expedition to Walcheren Island
where it lost far more men from dysentery than in battle. Perhaps
it was here that Joseph first suffered from the ague that was
eventually to discharge him. On their return to England they
were part of the great review on Brighton Downs, when Joseph
might have caught a glimpse of the Prince Regent and the future
William IV. Then it was back to the Peninsula for the great
battles of Salamanca and Vittoria and on across the Pyrenees
into France itself for Nivelle, Orthes and Toulouse.

After peace was made in France they were allowed a few days'
rest before embarking to take part in the war that was still going
on in Canada. At the end of this the battalion set out again for
France where Napoleon had reappeared, but didn't reach Paris
until August 24, 1815, thus missing Waterloo by a couple of
months, 'at once a disappointment and a misfortune,' as one
regimental historian put it, though in view of the casualties the
Fifth's rank and file might have felt differently.

Joseph Gilder had lived through the terrifying and brutal
episodes portrayed by Goya in 'Los Desastres de la Guerra'. He
had been fêted as a liberator. One private who, unlike Joseph,
could write told in a letter home of his disgust at being kissed by
men. He had seen soldiers so dead drunk on looted wine that
they lay like a stack of corpses. He had seen, as well as the
butchery of the bayonet charge, men hanged, women raped,
pillage and murder, troopers up to their knees in wine 'fighting
like tigers'.

Next came a bout as a member of the occupying army in
France, then home to England and three months later embarkation for the West Indies in February 1819. After five years'
service there Joseph was given his discharge at Dominica on
August 22, 1824, having served nineteen years and one hundred
and thirty-six days, 'in virtue of age, service and having had
repeated attacks of ague inducing visceral complaint'. His conduct
as a soldier had been 'good' and he was not, to his commanding
officer's knowledge, 'incapacitated by the sentence of a court
martial from receiving a pension'. He was forty-three years old,

147

Life in Thaxted must have seemed strange and monotonous after that of camp, barracks and the exotic West Indies but perhaps he welcomed the peace to repair his ravaged guts. Equally he must have been a heroic figure in the town, perhaps with a wound or two, his fresh complexion both tanned from the Caribbean sun and ensallowed by his 'visceral complaint'.

Soldiers were now common material for songs though some sang 'Sailors for my money'. Joseph wasn't the only one from the two families to enlist. John Jarvis had done his stint in the West Essex Militia, and the parish paid ten shillings a month to his wife while he was away in 1814, but he felt no call to the regular army life or if he did he resisted it.

Many changes had taken place in the Gilder family while Joseph was away. At some point his father James had died, certainly before 1810, when Joseph's stepmother Margaret is being described as Gilder widow of James to distinguish her from Mary widow of Henry. James must have been buried in a non-conformist graveyard. He can't have been more than forty-two. Margaret was helping to support herself by nursing for the parish. In July 1811 she was paid twelve shillings for one month's attendance at the pest house. Apart from sums of three to four shillings for nursing, she was paid a regular fourteen shillings a month until 1814 when it dropped to ten shillings and then through several steps until it was down to two shillings to half a crown in 1817.

It's possible that her two sons by James were helping to keep her by then, though it may be that they had died, since there's no sign of them in later records except for a clothing allowance for one of them in 1811. It's more likely that the price of bread had fallen and that the parish was implementing a more stringent policy in its outdoor relief, since Mary was also given two shillings a month in November and December 1815. Three months later she died aged eighty-five. To the family she had brought up alone it must have seemed like the end of an era. Her sister Elizabeth was still alive and receiving an occasional shilling.

In 1810 the overseers had had to make an allowance to 'paupers' because of the high price of flour. They had also had to pay Robert Jarvis's rent of thirty-five shillings. He and Martha had had thirteen children by 1809, four of whom were baptised in a clutch in 1799. One of his sons has the entry of fifteen shillings 'Mr Cornells clothing' which looks like an outfit for an apprenticeship in 1812. The following year Robert was bought a wheel but the account doesn't say of what type. Perhaps it was for Martha to augment the family income with spinning though there was little money to be earned that way now. Clare marks the shift from women spinning in the evening as they sat with their families to knitting or sewing in order not to have the time idle.

Robert had gone to Broxted as a labourer in the 1790s, where he married a girl called Martha Cole from Thaxted. He was described in the marriage register as 'sojourner'. Martha was put down by that name for the banns but as Mary for the marriage and their second child was christened at Thaxted as 'of Mary'. Perhaps she sometimes preferred to be a Mary rather than a Martha. A Robert Jarvis died and was buried in Broxted the year before their marriage. He is, I think, a missing Robert, son of Thomas and Grace, born in 1748 and therefore a likely father of this second Robert. The dates fit, and the names which Robert and Martha gave to their children, particularly their sons, which are old Jarvis names, including a Thomas and an Abraham. Clare documents the mobility of the labourers among the villages, a mobility lost to us now with the scarcity of homes. It had, as such things do, a good and a bad side. There is evidence in the registers of a constant desire to return home, to have the children christened there and to go home to die.

> The toil worn thresher, in his little cot
> Whose roof did shield his birth, and still remains
> His dwelling-place, how rough so e'er his lot,
> His toil though hard, and small the wage he gains
> That many a child most piningly maintains;
> Send him to distant scenes and better fare,
> How would his bosom yearn with parting pains;
> How would he turn and look, and linger there,
> And wish e'en now his cot and poverty to share.

Nowadays all classes expect to live mainly with their family of wife and children, however they may commute to the nearest town or even about the world, but then the labourers might be away for long periods of seasonal work.

Martin, another of Thomas and Grace's sons, was also finding it difficult to make ends meet. Now in his mid-fifties and probably with work hard to get or hard to do, he had his coat mended by the parish in 1811 and he was bought a shirt two years later for six shillings. Often these small disbursements preceded a death and Martin was buried in 1814. He is one of those shadows that have no substance from the cradle to the grave. There's no record of him marrying or having children, just his baptism, named from his mother's surname, his burial, aged fifty-six, a torn coat and a new shirt.

The price of Martin's shirt represented well over half a weekly wage for a labourer or twenty to thirty pounds at today's figure. The price of everything had risen during the century but although wages too had gone up from six to ten shillings a week they hadn't kept pace with costs, particularly of food. In real terms the labourers were worse off and there were far more of them, both because of the increase in population and because of the collapse of the small farms. The industrialisation of agriculture, which preceded that of industry itself, laid down a pattern of a large pool of labour of roughly equal skills and expectations. One labourer could be replaced by another without difficulty or retraining. The jobs in the countryside were more varied but the worker was expected to turn his hand to them all and if he couldn't someone else would, although Montague Burgoyne, the would-be Essex M.P. and landowner, complained to Arthur Young of the scarcity of labour and of ploughmen in particular and threatened to go over to sheep. This, though, was an artificial shortage, created by enlistment for the war with France.

Joseph Jarvis, the son of Patient and Mary, was in trouble too. A nurse was paid for by the parish at half a crown so he must have been ill, and his rent was paid several times. Paying the rent was a major problem because it had to be saved up for. If you had managed to survive to December but had put nothing by, Christmas might bring eviction. From the parish's point of view it was still probably cheaper to pay up than to take a whole family into the workhouse. The painful saving up of the rent must have been the origin of the old teapot or vase that served as a money-box on the mantelpieces of my childhood. The annual rent belonged to the old system of leases for tenants and wasn't suited to a weekly wage. In town, where there was no leasehold history, rents were collected weekly by the rentman. Still there remained the ten bob note for a rainy day or when visitors called unexpectedly and there was no money to buy them a drink.

Other Jarvisses came to the parish for help as the century got under way. What looks like a spinster Elizabeth, who would surely otherwise have been 'Widow Joseph' or some such, was helped with fairly large payments in some years, as was a William, another son of Thomas and Grace, and a Susan who had a large once-off payment of sixteen shillings in 1816 and may have been a daughter of Robert and Martha, going into service.

For this was another effect of the growing labouring class. The girls no longer stayed home to help their mothers with their side of the farm work and with the younger children. They went into service with the farmers and the rich shopkeepers and lesser gentry so that their wives and daughters need no longer bother with the physical work of the house. The mothers, left with a brood of small children, wept to see them go but were appeased by the money and presents they sent home, in particular, Flora Thompson records, their mistress's cast-offs. Thaxted girls first begin to be described as 'servant' at their marriages in the 1830s.

In theory it should have given them a greater experience of the world but in practice to work long hours for a local apothecary or farmer taught them nothing new. Even when they went right away to some big house, the worlds above and below stairs were so far apart that their lives weren't expanded except on the level of anecdote and an acquaintance with a variety of new material objects which made good gossip on a visit home. If there had been some attempt by their employers to teach them at least to read and write, the experience might have been more enriching but that no effort was made is evidenced by the numbers of servant girls who made their mark at their marriages.

Soldier Joseph's elder brother James had married, in 1812, a girl called Elizabeth Lilly. Their first children were christened in the parish church but later they joined other members of the family in having them baptised at the Independent Church. They had Mary-Ann the year of their marriage, Joseph, whose baptism isn't recorded in either church, in 1813 and John in 1817, Sarah a year later, Susan in 1820, Lydia in 1824, Rebecca the following year, Mahalah in 1831, by which time they had transferred allegiance to the Independents, and Elizabeth in

1836. Those are the ones who survived and who appear in the records. There may have been others. James lived in a cottage with a garden at Cutlers Green, where his cousin William was still managing to hang on to his farm. William and Rebecca's last recorded child, Peter, was born in 1807 but they may have had Timothy four years later, who died, aged two, in 1813.

Meanwhile Samuel Jarvis, the son of Robert and Martha, had married Susanne Perry at Lindsell in 1815 and their son Joseph had been born in 1817, the first of five children. The overseers of the poor at Lindsell had had Samuel up before them on his marriage and examined him, perhaps suspecting that he might be a burden on their rates. By the time his child was born he was back in Thaxted and living in a cottage with a garden at Bardfield End Green, as far out to the right of Thaxted as Cutlers Green was to the left, so that the two infant Josephs who were to be the fathers of Samuel and Lydia grew up as distant from each other as it was possible to be within the same parish, along the top arms of that starfish cluster of hamlets centring on the town.

The cottage gardens were vital to survival for they could provide the vegetables to supplement the basic diet of pudding, bread and a very little meat. By the middle of the century in response to the growing allotment movement, Lord Maynard had provided twenty-four acres of land for these, which further eked out the rations 'like the boy with his manners' as Maud still says. From the garden and allotment came the taste for 'greenery', as salads were called, that was transported to town to make the weekend teas of my childhood with cheese, ham or tinned fish. Tea remained, as in Flora Thompson's 'Lark Rise', the main meal of the day, eaten when we all got home at six and usually consisting of a batter or suet pudding, some sort of meat, potatoes and greens, laced if they were dark with vinegar that made them taste a little like winkles. Both Maud and her mother Minnie kept hens in their London backyards when they could, though when Maud was little the precious eggs went almost exclusively to father.

By 1821 Mary Gilder's sister, the Widow Jarvis, no longer even Widow William since all rivals had dropped away, was living in one of the row of almshouses, free from the fear of the workhouse, even though they had no plumbing and were only one room up and one down connected by very narrow stairs. She was receiving two shillings a week with an extra occasional sixpence for fuel, and about once a year a sum for clothes between half a crown and five and six. In July 1823 there began a series of casual payments that were probably for nursing or medicine. She died in November aged eighty-eight and the parish paid her funeral expenses of £1 . 10s . 6d, put down rather bizarrely under 'clothes', a reminder of the traditional grim joke about wooden overcoats.

The casual payments which were being made to Thomas and James Gilder, and Samuel and John, son of Joseph, Jarvis in 1823 and 1824 were commuted to a regular weekly allowance on April 25, 1825 and must be their make-up money from the poor rates of the difference between the labourer's low wage and the cost of living, the so-called Speenhamland system after the Berkshire parish where it was first introduced. At the same time Mary Gilder, James's aunt, who had been afflicted with fits from birth and therefore presumably unfit for service, was paid sixpence a week until October 1824 when payment suddenly stops with no explanation.

Samuel Jarvis also had his ten shillings a year rent paid and quite large sums every two or three months for clothes for his growing family. His allowance was high too at one and six a week. James Gilder's big family also meant higher payments for him but he owned the cottage where he lived, probably the last of great-grandfather William's legacy, and therefore didn't have to pay rent. Thomas, his uncle or more probably cousin William's son, and John Jarvis were topped up by ninepence a week and an occasional clothing allowance. Both Thomas and John had only two children to keep.

The whole town was going through a population leap after reaching what must have been an all-time low in 1811 when it fell to 1,733 and one hundred and eighty-one houses were uninhabited, over a third of the total. It must have looked like a ghost town. There had since been a rapid rise, with a great many births to bring the number of inhabitants to just over two thousand in 1821. Some people, like Thomas Gilder, who had married Dorothy Fitch and lived in Wimbish during the early days of his marriage, though bringing his children to Thaxted Independent Church to be baptised, now moved back to the town. There was a new industry too, straw plaiting, which

153

provided work for the women and children to take the place of the lost spinning.

There was also a new development or, rather, a renewal in the Gilder family which was a harbinger of things to come. William's youngest son Peter had learnt at least to write his name. I suspect that he had got a place in the Free School, once the old grammar school, where the master had been John Frye senior until 1819 when his son John, who had been drill sergeant for the Volunteers, took over. The year before he succeeded his father, a return to the House of Commons showed thirty boys and sixteen girls in attendance. Frye senior had many connections with John Jennings, the Independent Church minister, who was involved in starting the Thaxted Book Club and who was named as a trustee in Frye's will. Frye had attempted in 1800 to get the freedom to take the boys to the 'Meeting' for Sunday service as an alternative to the Parish Church but this was rejected by the charity Yardleys which was responsible for the school.

There was now a boarding school for the children of those who could afford it and there must have been at least a dame school or two. The first major educational effort for the poor was, however, not surprisingly in view of the connections I've noted above, made by the Independents when they built the British Schoolroom opposite the church in Bolford Street in 1849, just in time for Lydia's schooling. Wherever he learnt to do it, Peter signed his name at his marriage to Elizabeth Saward in 1826 but it wasn't until 1845 that any member of either family followed suit and then, rather surprisingly, it was a girl, Sussanah daughter of Joseph and Ann Jarvis.

Peter's brother William and sister Rebecca had both married in 1823 but they had made their marks. William was a labourer and he and his wife Mary Suckling had a cottage and garden rented from one of her farmer relatives in Cutlers Green, near the rest of the Gilder family. Soldier Joseph, who by 1844 was living in a tenement belonging to the vicar, Thomas Jee, in the town itself, had also been living in Cutlers Green three years before. Ten years after his discharge from the army he had married Rebecca Glascock. Joseph must have recovered his health and kept a fairly youthful appearance for the compiler of the 1841 census put him down as three years younger than his age. Perhaps he had fudged it a bit when he married Rebecca, who

154

was eighteen years his junior.

Peter Gilder's new-won literacy made no difference to his status. He too was a labourer. There's no record of any children for him and his first wife Elizabeth, who died in 1837 aged thirty. Six months later he married Susan Francis and their children were baptised in the parish church. It's possible that Emma, aged two, buried in 1830, is his daughter but she may also be a child of his brother John, none of whose children's births are recorded. The brothers seemed to move between the Established and Non-conformist sects.

Their mother Rebecca died in 1835 and their father William a year later although he had been fourteen years older than his wife according to his burial entry, though only ten according to his baptismal record. Perhaps he liked to pose as older than he was or had genuinely forgotten. It must have been then that William's property Hows Hall Farm passed to John and he was able to be described in 1841 as farmer. His new wife's name was Sarah and living with them at that date they had a daughter Louisa, aged twenty, and sons Jonathan and Peter aged fifteen who should be twins. John and Sarah had only been married a few months. She was a widow and her father's profession was soldier. His name was Lawrence Unwin, the acceptable modification that had taken the place of the earlier Onion. Brother Peter Gilder and his wife Susan were witnesses at the wedding, an evidence of how close the families kept.

The Jarvisses too kept close, so much so that three of the daughters of Joseph and Elizabeth married Townsend boys. But brothers and sisters marrying their in-laws was common. In a small place it was hard to meet new people. The social environment could both reinforce and obscure any incestuous drives. Sometimes, too, families were intermarrying who had already done so a hundred years before. Although new names were added to the town the old ones persisted with great tenacity, showing that the Jarvisses and Gilders weren't alone or even unusual in staying put.

By 1841 there were nine Jarvis households and six Gilder. There were also four Jarvis girls out to service in other people's houses in and around the town, and three Gilders. Their employers included farmers, a miller, two brothers who were 'druggists', a grocer and draper, and an auctioneer. One of the

Jarvis boys, Thomas, was living-in with young Will Stally who, although the same age, was described as farmer, a brave attempt that had collapsed a few years later. The most important of the young men from the point of view of the eventual birth of Samuel Jarvis, his father Joseph, wasn't at home when the census was taken and must have been working away. However, there was no lack of a Joseph for there were at least five others ranging in age from seventy-five to four. One of them had managed to break out of the labouring rut and was a shoemaker.

Seven years later a John Jarvis had become a bonnet trimming manufacturer, presumably as an adjunct to the straw plait industry. His son Joseph was carrying the trade on in 1855 and his son John was a draper and grocer in the sixties. Joseph Jarvis of Bardfield Green ran a beerhouse in 1848. But both these efforts outside labouring were exhausted by the 1870s. Only Peter Gilder, the son of farmer John, still held on at Hows Hall into the eighties.

Joseph Gilder, the father-to-be of Lydia, was living at home with his parents and two of his sisters in 1841. The following year he married Sarah Stally who had been in service and seven years later his sister Mahalah married Sarah's brother Daniel. I'm glad that somewhere in one of the families occurs that uniquely Essex name for a girl which was to provide the title and name of the heroine for Sabine Baring-Gould's *Romance of the Essex Marshes*. Mahalah too had been in service. Joseph and Sarah were witnesses at their wedding.

Three years before, Joseph Jarvis had married Sarah Drane. Although both Josephs and Sarahs were married at the parish church neither couple brought their children there to be baptised. Both Josephs were labourers, the sons of labourers and their Sarahs were the daughters of labourers. None of them could sign their names.

It was, I believe, at this period that the homogeneous working-class culture that stretched certainly from the Midlands to the Channel, and from the North Sea to the Bristol Channel, was evolved, a survival culture ground out of poverty. Intensely conservative and materialistic, this culture, which still affects our lives and attitudes in many ways is nevertheless very little understood or even acknowledged. Transported to London with the flood of agricultural labourers in the nineteenth century, it

156

became the ethos of the respectable metropolitan working class which Maud, and I in my turn, was to grow up in. When I was evacuated to Wiltshire in the Second World War, I found it duplicated there, down to the children's singing games.

The very phrases and idioms used by Flora Thompson's 'Lark Rise' inhabitants were everyday usage with us fifty years later, and in town not country. There were some variations of syntax and vocabulary, beloved of linguists, and these have often been allowed to obscure the depth of the similarity. Upon a small basic vocabulary were grafted stock expressions that were pushed out like coloured symbols to express stock responses. The coming of universal schooling made no real dent in this essentially pre-literate oral culture but existed alongside it providing merely a useful tool that by and large was handled less well than the ones the new scholars were used to in home and field. It was handy to be able to write to families away, to read a newspaper for national gossip. The women also read the tuppenny novelette, always referred to as 'my book', the forerunner of the women's magazines. Lydia was a great consumer of these in her old age. But even this wasn't allowed to really influence the imagination, for the culture was anti-imaginative and anti-sensitive. Such things could only soften the will and possibly the brain. Too much thinking, it was believed, sent people mad. It certainly made them less able to cope with the constant struggle to live, in which there was no room for mistakes which might consume a week's baking or a hard-won piece of clothing.

It was hard, like the conditions that gave it birth, tough and often hypocritical because it was concerned to keep up appearances, to cover up poverty, to hide any opinions that might endanger a job or a roof over the family's head. It developed a rough satire for use behind the farmer's or the bailiff's back and a way of looking at things to minimise them with a half joke because they must be endured not changed. It made ideal soldiers for trench warfare or ideal civilians to suffer a blitz.

Its aim was material comfort and here it has its roots both in eighteenth-century materialism and in the yeoman values. It is also strongly resistant to change, except of the fashionable kind in clothes and consumer goods. The fear of change comes from a century of development when every new idea, like the threshing machine, meant lost jobs or lowered wages, and this fear is a continuing reality. At the same time the culture is against personal aggrandisement or competition. Those who do 'get on' must be careful to keep the same ways and speech and not to try and 'come it' over those who haven't been moved by their education into a different class, as many of Samuel and Lydia's descendants would eventually be with the chance of more than primary schooling.

The unrest among farmworkers throughout the country in the 1830s touched Essex too, and its violent suppression further encouraged a self-preserving hypocrisy, particularly in political beliefs. The workhouse still loomed as the ultimate punishment for those who couldn't keep up but it was no longer even in Thaxted. Instead there was the Dunmow Union Poor House where one of the Robert Jarvisses died aged eighty-two in 1843. Perhaps it was the husband of Martha whose funeral the parish had paid thirty shillings and sixpence for in 1820. The workhouse was said to be run on very liberal lines and allowed the inmates a choice of Non-conformist or Established service on Sunday.

The coming of the railway to Essex, but bypassing the town, further deepened the decline that Thaxted had slipped into like one of its own daughters: a cousin of Lydia named Lydia Gilder, for instance, who died in 1849 aged eighteen. A writer at the end of the century described the country around as 'bare of woods, of timber even, and of streams. The unclothed hillsides lie in long furrows of tilled land. Year by year a crop of indifferent grain is their output, and each summer now beholds more acres yielded to the untutored growth of weeds . . . The most picturesque feature of the landscape is to be found in the delapidated windmills which crown many of the summits . . . Thaxted probably reached the lowest period of its stagnation about twenty years ago. Then, the chance visitor who entered its silent and deserted streets beheld houses uninhabited, chapels shut up, huge maltings and granaries falling into decay'.

Into this decay Samuel Jarvis was born in 1848, to be followed by his wife-to-be Lydia Gilder five years later. His birth coincided with the presentation to Lydia's great-uncle, soldier Joseph, of the General Service Medal with five clasps for the five great battles of the Peninsular War in which he had fought with the

158

Fighting Fifth. In spite of the poverty and dilapidation, he had come home to marry a local girl and die. I wonder if he kept his medal or was forced to sell it, whether he became a bore with his tales of distant lands and battles or whether he was a hero again to his community when the medal arrived.

Robert Jarvis also came home from the Dunmow poor house to be buried in the parish graveyard and lie among three centuries of ancestors. So it wasn't perhaps surprising that Samuel and Lydia in their turn should one day come back, though the town they had left was that of 'the lowest period of its stagnation'. Their youngest son Harry, now himself a grandfather, and my great-uncle, puts it quite simply and rightly when I ask him why: 'They were bred and born there, duck, bred and born.'

ENDNOTE

Much of the material which formed the basis of this study is to be found in the Essex Record Office in Chelmsford and I must express my thanks to the staff, and to Mrs Wendy Stubbings for her help in sifting through it. The Society of Genealogists also provided much valuable material and my thanks are due to the staff there, and to the Public Record Office for the use of its facilities and records. Above all I am grateful for the personal recollections of Mrs Maud Williamson and Mr Harry Jarvis.

The quotations in verse are largely drawn from folksongs and the poems of John Clare.